POP-11
PROGRAMMING
FOR ARTIFICIAL
INTELLIGENCE

INTERNATIONAL COMPUTER SCIENCE SERIES

Consulting editors **A D McGettrick** University of Strathclyde
J van Leeuwen University of Utrecht

OTHER TITLES IN THE SERIES:

Programming in Ada (2nd Edn.) *J G P Barnes*

Computer Science Applied to Business Systems *M J R Shave and K N Bhaskar*

Software Engineering (2nd Edn.) *I Sommerville*

A Structured Approach to FORTRAN 77 Programming *T M R Ellis*

The Cambridge Distributed Computing System *R M Needham and A J Herbert*

An Introduction to Numerical Methods with Pascal *L V Atkinson and P J Harley*

The UNIX System *S R Bourne*

Handbook of Algorithms and Data Structures *G H Gonnet*

Office Automation: Concepts, Technologies and Issues *R A Hirschheim*

Microcomputers in Engineering and Science *J F Craine and G R Martin*

UNIX for Super-Users *E Foxley*

Software Specification Techniques *N Gehani and A D McGettrick* (eds.)

Data Communications for Programmers *M Purser*

Local Area Network Design *A Hopper, S Temple and R C Williamson*

Prolog Programming for Artificial Intelligence *I Bratko*

Modula-2: Discipline & Design *A H J Sale*

Introduction to Expert Systems *P Jackson*

Prolog *F Giannesini, H Kanovi, R Pasero and M van Caneghem*

Programming Language Translation: A Practical Approach *P D Terry*

System Simulation: Programming Styles and Languages *W Kreutzer*

Data Abstraction in Programming Languages *J M Bishop*

The UNIX System V Environment *S R Bourne*

The Craft of Software Engineering *A Macro and J Buxton*

UNIX℠ is a trademark of AT & T Bell Laboratories.

POP-11
PROGRAMMING
FOR ARTIFICIAL
INTELLIGENCE

Mike Burton
Nigel Shadbolt

University of Nottingham

ADDISON-WESLEY
PUBLISHING
COMPANY

Wokingham, England · Reading, Massachusetts · Menlo Park, California
Don Mills, Ontario · Amsterdam · Bonn · Sydney · Singapore
Tokyo · Madrid · Bogota · Santiago · San Juan

Cover graphic by kind permission of Apollo Computer Inc.
Photo-typset at the University of Nottingham.
Printed in Great Britain by The Bath Press.

British Library Cataloguing in Publication Data

Burton, Mike
  Pop-11 programming for artificial
  intelligence.–(International computer
  science series)
  1. Artificial intelligence–Data
  processing   2. Pop-11 (Computer program
  language)
  I. Title   II. Shadbolt, Nigel   III. Series
  006.3'02855133   Q336

  ISBN 0-201-18049-9

Library of Congress Cataloging in Publication Data

Burton, Mike, 1959–
  POP-11 programming for artificial intelligence.

  (International computer science series)
  Bibliography; p.
  Includes index.
  1. Artificial intelligence–Data processing.
2. POP (Computer program language)   I. Shadbolt, Nigel,
1956–   . II. Title. III. Title: POP-eleven programming for artificial intelligence. IV. Series.
Q336.B88 1987   006.3'028'55133   86-32059
ISBN 0-201-18049-9

To Vicki
and
To Beverly

Preface

This book serves two purposes. In Part One we provide an introductory course in the programming language POP-11. In Part Two we show how POP-11 can be used to develop artificial intelligence (AI) programs. We do this by building parts of classic AI programs and discussing their relevance to the discipline as a whole. The book should thus be taken as a course in *practical* AI.

The course, as presented here, has grown out of our experiences in teaching AI to psychology undergraduates. In POP-11 we found a language which is sufficiently easy to learn and at the same time has sufficient power to build genuinely interesting programs. While POP-11 has a great deal of documentation associated with it, we felt the need for a structured text. Therefore we have aimed to produce a course in the language rather than a complete description of its full capabilities. No programming experience is assumed and though, of course, we had psychological applications in mind when writing, we believe that the text will be of use to the increasing number of people turning to computer modelling in many fields.

In our AI chapters we hope to plug another gap. Most texts on AI provide a coverage of *what* has been done, without saying *how* the programs can be realized. In building small, but real, AI programs we take the reader through the relevant steps and end up with working programs. This is what we mean in saying that we aim to provide a course in practical AI.

Almost everyone who uses POP-11 will do so as part of the POPLOG system. POPLOG is a programming environment consisting of three languages (POP-11, PROLOG and LISP), an editor (VED) and a great deal of on-line documentation. The documentation ranges from very simple introductory articles, to formal descriptions of the internal workings of POP-11. In Appendix C we provide readers with an outline guide to POPLOG and point to on-line documentation which may be useful.

Many people have contributed to this book in a variety of ways. First of all we must thank Roger Henry and Hugh Smith for introducing us to POP-11 in the first place. These two have commented on early drafts of the book, as have Vicki Bruce, Aaron Sloman and a number of anonymous reviewers. It goes without saying that we claim responsibility for any blunders still present. Penny Lightburn provided willing secretarial support, and Simon Plumtree gave sound editorial advice. In the final stages, George Paechter was most helpful in performing the typesetting.

Perhaps our final word of thanks should go to our students, who have never been slow to criticize any flaw in our didactic style. Their criticism has contributed substantially to this book.

Mike Burton and Nigel Shadbolt
July 1986

Contents

Trademark notices

A number of programming languages and expert system shells mentioned in this book are available commercially, and the following trademarks apply: SMALLTALK and LOOPS are trademarks of Xerox Corporation; KEE is a trademark of Intellicorp; SAVOIR is a trademark of ISI Ltd; ESP ADVISOR is a trademark of Expert Systems International; and Xi is a trademark of Expertech.

Chapter 1 Artificial Intelligence and Computational Modelling

1.1 Introduction

Thirty years ago a small conference was held at Dartmouth College in the United States. The delegates included computer scientists, psychologists, linguists and philosophers. They met to discuss the computer simulation of intelligence. In 1956 this seemed no more than a dream. Computers were in their infancy, the hardware and software was primitive. No one understood the nature of what was to be simulated. The field of enquiry did not even have a name. By the time the conference ended one thing at least had changed; John McCarthy had coined the term 'Artificial Intelligence'.

Today rather more has changed. Computers are thousands of times more powerful whilst the cost of hardware continues to plummet. The programs running on today's machines are hugely more sophisticated than their distant forbears. Furthermore, we now understand rather more about the processes which support intelligent behaviour. These developments have, in part, contributed to the emergence of artificial intelligence (AI) as a science in its own right.

This book is aimed at students who need to understand the process of AI modelling, and in particular cognitive modelling. It is divided into two parts. The first is an introduction to programming in POP-11. It provides a course in the 'nuts and bolts' of the language without much reference to AI applications. It is not a complete and exhaustive description of the language. Rather the aim is to provide an understanding of the most important concepts in POP-11.

The second part presents POP-11 as an AI modelling tool. Various AI techniques and applications which have captured the imagination of the academic community, are discussed, and aspects of these are presented as examples, exercises and projects.

The emphasis throughout is on POP-11 as a tool for AI modelling, not as an abstract formal construction. For this reason the book will also be of interest to those in industry and commerce exploring the possibilities of AI for the first time.

1.2 AI in context

As hardware and software developed through the late fifties and early sixties, AI work gathered momentum. This has resulted in a proliferation of applications and techniques. Application areas include vision, natural language understanding, robotics and expert systems. AI techniques comprise methods for searching 'problem spaces', planning sequences of actions to solve problems, methods of reasoning and deduction, and techniques for representing knowledge. Any particular application will typically call on numerous AI methods and techniques. Historically a proportion of AI research has been application driven whilst other work has looked at extending the available methods and techniques.

One of the earliest application areas was machine translation. Early optimism that a simple solution could be found was soon dashed. It was not sufficient to look up word by word a passage of Russian to generate an English equivalent. Much more substantial knowledge was required by the system. This included ways of representing the rules of syntax and semantics (rules of grammar and meaning). The principled inclusion of knowledge into a system is a distinguishing feature of AI applications. Moreover, such applications require the development of new methods and techniques. Research into machine translation, for example, led to many new techniques for parsing – the systematic analysis of strings of symbols into constituents according to a set of grammatical principles.

Many application areas attempted to integrate various AI subsystems, for example, visual and robotic systems. The famous SHAKEY system, a robot developed at the Stanford Research Institute, was able to perform elementary visual analysis, and to work out ways of moving in and acting on its environment. Another integrative project was Winograd's (1973) SHRDLU system, a simulated robot with problem solving abilities which included some natural language understanding.

Such systems might appear very humble given the expectations generated by Hollywood stars such as HAL, C3PO and R2D2! However one of the most enduring lessons of AI has been to increase our respect for 'mundane intelligence'. While the solutions to artificial 'perception' and 'comprehension' are still far from satisfactory, many activities which we prize as intellectual the machines have found easy. Playing chess, solving problems in crypto-arithmetic, solving differential equations are all behaviours which can now be accomplished by machine. Why is this? Much of it has to do with a property of these domains sometimes called the 'closed world assumption'.

AI has progressed largely inasmuch as it has restricted itself to 'closed worlds' or 'micro-worlds'. To illustrate a closed world, consider the Tower of Hanoi problem (Figure 7.1, page 84). In this closed world we have three posts and a set of discs with holes in them, each disc has a different radius. At the start of the problem all of the discs are on one post, each disc resting on the one just bigger than it. The task is to move all of the discs to one of the other posts. Only a single disc may be moved at a time and all the other discs must be on one of the posts. At no time during the process of solving the problem may a disc be placed on top of a disc that is smaller than it. The third post can be used as a temporary resting place for the discs. This problem gets increasingly difficult the larger the number of discs used.

The domain described has a fixed starting point and a determinate goal state. It has a fixed number of rules which specify how moves can be made. In fact one can, in principle, enumerate all the possible moves in any Tower of Hanoi problem. What one needs is a systematic way of searching this set of moves (or 'problem space') to find the goal state. Much of the power of AI resides in providing ways of searching only that part of the space which contains moves likely to provide a solution.

As we can see, closed worlds in problem solving have an enumerable set of states, well understood start and end states, and a finite set of rules or legal actions which will move one through the problem space. Closed worlds were the starting point in many successful AI applications. Winograd's SHRDLU system had a small number of objects to manipulate, a small repertoire of actions, limited methods of planning, and understood only a 'restricted' set of the English language. Restricted in the sense that the grammar accounted for a small set of the permissible sentences in English and the meanings of the terms were fixed.

Once we move outside a micro-world and abandon the closed world assumption things become very much harder. In the generalized problem of visual recognition we cannot assume, as early systems did, that all objects in the world are rectilinear, that lighting is uniform, that objects are stationary and so on. The general case is 'recognize scene X'. This type of task is one we perform without much conscious reflection – this is 'mundane intelligence'. AI has demonstrated that we should respect it.

What makes the generalized cases so hard? We have already hinted at some of the problems – these are simply the converse of closed world properties. There are many objects in the domains of interest, some of which will not have been experienced before. The relationships and properties of these objects are numerous and vague. Contingencies or rules in the domain do not always hold reliably – there may often be exceptions to any rules that do exist. Faced with an 'open world', how do we cope? How do intelligent systems succeed in dealing with the natural environment? This brings us to another distinction which has become evident in the course of AI research. The contrast between so-called 'weak' and 'strong' methods.

Much of the early work in AI was aimed at developing a battery of 'weak methods'. These methods were general mechanisms which could be applied to numerous domains – they were not 'strongly' tied to the particulars of a domain, nor dependent on strong assumptions about knowledge of that domain. Good examples of this are some of the search algorithms described in Chapter 7. In contrast, methods which utilize specific knowledge about the domain are known as 'strong AI methods'.

The search for a set of weak methods capable of providing the general foundations of intelligent behaviour was in the end frustrated. Weak methods work reasonably well in closed domains but not on real world problems. When we solve problems and act on our environment we use a great deal of knowledge about the world; how it is structured, what actions are appropriate in what circumstances, what exceptional cases might arise. In short, our problem solving is immensely context determined. There seems to be no universal theory of problem solving or knowledge representation which underlies everything else.

The lessons of AI have been important in shaping our understanding of the character of human intelligence. Nevertheless, we must beware of expecting too much. AI is furnishing a tool-box of methods and techniques which provide ways of exploring cognitive processes. It is not about to deliver the millennial Theory of Psychology neatly wrapped and packed.

The principal research tool which AI offers psychology is that of computational modelling – models of the possible processes of cognition. And it is to the question of models and modelling that we now turn.

1.3 Commonsense models

What do we mean by a model? A good place to start to answer this question is to look at our commonsense notion of a model. What does one think of when one hears the word model? Possible candidates include: the model aeroplanes made by children; the scale models made by architects for display to clients; the balsa wood bridges that school children make as part of their school physics curriculum. These three models fulfill different purposes. Model aeroplanes are meant to be played with, the client can understand the layout of his new housing estate by looking at the scale model, and the bridges are built only to be destroyed by hanging weights from them in order to test their strength.

What characteristics do these three disparate examples share which make them all candidates for our normal use of the term model? They are all representations of the modelled objects, they maintain certain of the original's characteristics and not others. The decision as to what is and is not represented depends on what the model is to be used for.

Consider the architect's scale model. The characteristics it will share with the final estate are quite easy to name. The relative distances between landmarks will be the same in model and world; buildings will retain the same relative positions; hills and depressions will share the same relative heights and the same slopes. This model then, serves the purpose of allowing one to inspect the estate at a glance, and to establish the relative positions of various elements.

Now consider the possibility that we might use the model for another purpose. Suppose we want to build another house on some unoccupied site. The model will provide a certain amount of information, e.g. how far the site is from other buildings, and so forth. However, we certainly cannot start construction on the basis of this information. Certain aspects of the world will not be represented in this model, e.g. where underground power cables lie, what the soil type is on our site, etc. In fact, an altogether different model would be needed for this project, or perhaps a collection of different types of models.

The moral of the example is simply this: there are often very many different models available (or possible) as representations of the same modelled thing. Which model one decides to use, or build, depends entirely on what one wants to use it for. A pen with a ruler lain across it may be a perfectly good model of an aeroplane for some purposes, whereas for different purposes one may need a model which looks and flies like the real thing. There is nothing magical about a model – it simply represents certain aspects of something else.

So far we have only considered physical models – but a model does not have to be a physical object. A model can be made of words, for instance. Consider the following model of a train.

A train is a long tubular vehicle which travels along iron rails at speeds of 0 to 125 m.p.h. A train may carry passengers who may embark and alight only at railway stations.

This model of a train may be adequate for certain purposes. For instance, if we wish to know how fast trains travel we can consult this model, and discover that the range is 0 to 125 m.p.h. However, just as with the models mentioned above, this one only has a limited usefulness and will not help us if we want to know how to design a faster train.

All of the models considered so far are models of the physical characteristics of objects, they are **structural** models. There is another, very important type, and this is called a **functional** model. An easy (though rather oversimplified) way to think of this distinction is that a structural model represents what something *is*, whereas a functional model represents what something *does*. Consider the following model of a thermostat for instance. This is the type of device used in the boiler of a central heating or hot water system.

Step 1. Check the temperature of the water.

Step 2. If the temperature is above the required level, then do nothing.

Step 3. If the temperature is below the required level, then apply heat to the boiler.

Step 4. Start again at Step 1.

This is an interesting model of a dynamic process – one which changes all the time. The boiler operates in the following way; if after a check the temperature is found to be above the required level, the mechanism does not apply heat – thus allowing the water to cool down. If, on a subsequent check, the temperature has fallen below the criterion level, then it is heated up. The temperature inside the boiler then, is not constant, but constantly fluctuating around the criterion temperature. The amount of this fluctuation will depend upon how long it takes to go through the four steps, how quickly water cools down, how much heat is applied in Step 3, and so forth. These are not values that we know, but nevertheless the model does provide insight into the workings of a simple thermostat. Moreover, it includes no information about how a thermostat is built, what it looks like, or how its parts are connected to one another. This is a functional model – it represents the functions rather than the structure of a thermostat.

Let's take stock of what we have learnt by considering various simple sorts of everyday model. A model is a representation of something, it preserves certain characteristics of the original, whilst ignoring certain others. Exactly which characteristics are preserved is left to the builder or user of that model. A model can be a physical object, or a more abstract representation – such as a description in ordinary English. Furthermore, the thing modelled can be a physical object, or some abstract process.

When we talk of 'formal models' in cognitive science and AI we are using the same underlying ideas we have discussed here. The difference is that we wish to be very precise about what each part of the model means. We will look in more detail at how formal models aim to do this.

1.4 Formal models

Models are essentially representations. To understand our models or representations we must be clear about the following:

1. What is the medium of representation?
2. What is the original object we are trying to represent?
3. What aspects of the medium are doing the representing?
4. What aspects of the original do we want to model?
5. What are the precise correspondences between elements of the model and the original?

The modelling mediums we have looked at so far have been various, ranging from physical components in the scale model, to explicit languages in the case of the thermostat and the train. In each case the medium of modelling or representation possesses certain constituents which are placed into correspondences with certain features of the object or process being modelled.

Now, we can regard the modelling medium as having a structure itself. The clearer and more precise this structure the better able it will be to represent in a clear and precise manner those features of the original which we wish to represent.

A modelling medium with which we are all familiar is the language of simple mathematics. Let us consider a very elementary formal model – a simple algebraic model. Suppose we take the expression '$x = y/z$'. What are the constituents of this expression? There are the variables x, y and z which we know, via the conventions of this medium, can take ranges of values. There is the concept of division and the concept of an equivalence relation.

This formal expression can serve as a model. This is done by providing a mapping between the things in the medium and the objects in the real world we wish to model. Let us suppose that x is the current value of a bicycle, z is the age of the bicycle and y is the price of the equivalent bicycle brand new. We can propose the algebraic expression as a model for a property of the real world. Namely, a relationship between the age, value, and new price of a particular bicycle. The older the bicycle, the less value it has as a proportion of its price brand new.

Now we have no idea whether this is a good model, whether it reflects a real underlying relationship between the quantities. That is for the model builder to demonstrate by using the model against known data. It is likely that this model suffers from all sorts of weaknesses – it may oversimplify, it may leave out crucial features by not including enough variables. However, it remains a model, whether good or bad.

A further interesting feature of formal modelling mediums is that we can use them and interpret them in very different ways. Indeed in the extreme case we can use the same construction in the medium of representation to represent something else entirely. Our simple algebraic model could be used for instance to model the effect of some drug. Let x be the level of the drug in the bloodstream, y represents the amount of the drug administered and z represents the patient's weight.

When a particular model is able to sustain a wide range of interpretations we might be tempted to speculate that we have modelled some common law or process which underlies a variety of different real world situations. So for example we can imagine a generalized version of our model of a thermostat which could be seen as underlying any regulatory process.

Step 1. Check the value of some property of the object.

Step 2. If this value is above the required level, then do nothing.

Step 3. If this value is below the required level, then apply some process to increase the property's value.

Step 4. Start again at Step 1.

The key concept to appreciate in this section is that we can use formal mediums to build models. We can think of formal mediums as formal languages of representation. They are formal because they are precise and well understood; they allow us to build precise and unambiguous models. Of course, these models may simplify reality. Indeed, there is an interesting relation between the problem of modelling and the closed world assumption. In the course of learning about modelling you will doubtless come to your own conclusions about this relationship, and the limitations and problems inherent in modelling.

1.5 AI models

AI is often characterized as the attempt to build **computational models** of intelligent processes. How do computational models relate to the ideas we have been discussing in the last two sections? The link is to be found in the concept of programming languages.

A program is simply a set of commands which a computer can inter- pret and act upon. The program is built out of a programming language. Programming languages have all the properties which formal mediums of representation have. In turn the programs built out of programming languages are computational embodiments of models. A computer model is no different from any other model mentioned so far. A computer model is a representation in a formal language (a programming language) of some object or process.

The art of AI modelling consists of the ability to specify the problem to be solved – once this has been done, the programming is usually easy. It is a matter of translating the specification into a particular programming language.

Specification is at the heart of computer modelling. When learning to program, the student soon becomes aware of just how little a computer can be assumed to 'know'. Things which are obvious to the programmer have to be specified to the computer. Of course, this is one of the argu- ments in favour of AI. One often comes to a problem with a solution one considers quite plausible. When programmed, it turns out that the machine needs more information – perhaps because one has assumed some knowledge, or glossed over some difficulties hidden by the ambiguity of the terms in one's original solution. A computer is a 'dumb machine', and the rigour this enforces on its operator illustrates its power as a model- ling tool.

As an example of the specification process, consider the following problem. This problem is a form of geometric analogy problem solving and was first formalized in an AI program by Evans (1968). How has P in Figure 1.1 been changed to produce Q; use the rule to find the analogous change for R into one of the set S–V.

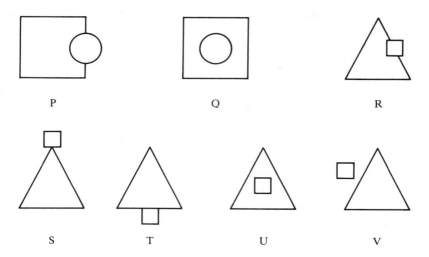

Figure 1.1 A geometric analogy problem.

What we must do here is give:

1. A description of P.
2. A description of Q.
3. Compare these descriptions – what must be done to produce Q from P?
4. A description of R.
5. Apply Step 3 to produce one of S–V from R.

We can refine this specification by using structural descriptions of the figures and comparing them.

1. P is 'a square with a circle on its perimeter'.
2. Q is 'a square with a circle inside it'.
3. Change 'on its perimeter' to 'inside it'.
4. R is 'a triangle with a square on its perimeter'.
5. Solution is 'a triangle with a square inside it'.

From this specification it is a small step to programming the solution in an appropriate programming language.

This brings us on to the question of what language to use for AI modelling. There are, of course, many different programming languages in use throughout the world. This being so, it is worth considering where POP-11 stands in relation to the rest.

According to what exactly one wants to do with a computer, various programming languages are better at certain jobs than others. Obviously one attempts to select a programming language which offers a natural way of modelling and manipulating the problem area.

Consider some algebraic problem which a mathematician wishes to solve. If the terms, operations and so forth, of a particular programming language resemble in some way the notational form of algebra, it will be easier for the mathematician to formulate the program in this language, than in one which did not have these properties. In fact, the various ALGOL languages provide just such tools.

Modelling mathematical problems is not the principal interest of AI. Researchers in AI are concerned to represent knowledge in more general ways. Consider the following problem which might confront researchers wanting to make a start at analysing natural language:

Which words are nouns in the following sentence: 'The green book lay unopened on the table.'?

A first stab at a specification for this problem might be as follows.

1. Make a list of words and call it 'nouns'. This list might include the words: cat house book dog table ... .

2. Make a list of the words in the sentence and call it 'sentence'.

3. Take the first word of 'sentence' and check whether it is in the list called 'nouns'.

4. If the word is in 'nouns' then print it out. If the word is not in 'nouns' then don't do anything.

5. Repeat Steps 3 and 4 for the next word in 'sentence'.

It is obvious that for this kind of problem, a mathematical language would be quite inappropriate. For this reason, languages were developed which incorporated such notions as words, lists of words, and so on. Amongst these languages are LISP (a popular American LISt Processing language) and POP-11. Just as with the example above, AI languages offer ways of building structural descriptions of the sort required for our Geometry Analogy Solver.

POP-11 is a suitable programming language for AI because it is often appropriate for the kinds of problems that people in these areas wish to study. POP-11 is in no absolute sense better or worse than other languages – it is simply very useful for certain kinds of problem.

Finally in discussing AI models we should note that cognitive modelling is a subset of AI modelling. The aim of AI is to produce programs which perform tasks which would require intelligence if performed by humans. For certain types of problems in AI, there is no attempt to make one's programs work *in the same way* as we think that humans work. As opposed to this, in cognitive modelling we are explicitly trying to offer an account of how humans solve problems, represent knowledge or whatever.

1.6 Modelling – the pros and cons

The modelling process is at once both simple and profound. The immediate concept is straightforward. To understand how modelling provides us with insights is more difficult. Nevertheless, what can we say about the advantages and disadvantages of modelling as they pertain to psychology? When you lay down a specification of a process and then attempt to model it you quickly realize that there are a number of ways in which you must evaluate your model.

In the first instance you must ask whether your model is *consistent*. A model is consistent if it does not generate contradictions, if its various components fit together so as to form a coherent whole. We can also ask if our model is *complete*. Does the specification cover the range of cases we wish to model, does it have the scope we need? A further feature, one which is hard to define absolutely has to do with what we might term *elegance*. Does the model represent the original in an elegant fashion, have we captured the general principles without too many special exceptions, or have we had to resort to little bits and pieces which make it work but which have no realization in the original? We can also see if our model is *superficial*. To what extent have simplifying assumptions been made which simplify away crucial problems? Further, we can ask if the model is *predictive*. Does it generate novel behaviour which nevertheless seems reasonable? This often arises out of computational models which have a degree of complexity and generality. Indeed the ability of computational models to reveal the consequences of complex changing processes is a feature which no pen and paper model can easily convey. Finally, we should consider whether the model is capable of *refutation*, can it be lain against the original and said to be adequate or inadequate, right or wrong?

There are some additional dangers to note. One is the danger of believing that a feature of the medium of representation is important in the original when really it is not there at all. And there is simply the danger of being over-impressed by the existence of a computational model at all.

Having added these caveats it is worth making one last important point. Psychology has a tenuous understanding of the nature of some of its most important concepts. What are representations? What does a cognitive process consist of? The challenge of AI is in part to make us face the issue of representation head on. In building models of cognitive processes we are asking what are possible classes of representations, what are their limits, what are their consequences.

In this chapter we have introduced you to the aims and scope of this book. It is our intention to introduce you to the basics of AI modelling, with POP-11 as our chosen modelling medium.

The next few chapters describe the basic components of POP-11. We then introduce some basic AI methods used in modelling search, knowledge representation, planning and natural language processing. This is not the place to catalogue the current state of the art in AI. This is left to our final chapter, where the future for both AI and POP-11 is discussed.

Part One

A Course in POP-11

Chapter 2 **The Building Blocks of POP-11**

2.1 Introduction

In any programming language (indeed in natural language) there are rules about what is meaningful and what is not. As in ordinary language, POP-11 has a 'vocabulary', a set of names which mean something in that language. Furthermore, there are rules about how that vocabulary may be used – as in ordinary language, the rules of combination are referred to as 'syntax'. In this chapter, we will introduce some of the most common vocabulary of POP-11, and talk about the ways in which it is used.

POP-11 is an interactive language. This means that it will accept instructions which you type onto the terminal, and provide you with any appropriate 'output' then and there. You can specify this output to a certain extent, but POP-11 will sometimes provide you with output you weren't expecting – usually in the form of MISHAP messages. You will become familiar with these messages, and realize just how helpful they are as you progress through this course.

The best way to get a feel for a language like POP-11 is to sit at a computer terminal and experiment with the language. When you come to write large programs you will want to avoid going to the computer without preparatory work, but initially you need to become acquainted with the system. Login to your computer and access POP-11 (usually by typing pop11 – though this may vary between machines). You will get a message on your screen, telling you which version of POP-11 you are using, possibly some other information, and then a colon prompt like this

```
:
```

This colon means that POP-11 is now ready to receive some instructions. Whatever you choose to type at this stage is a computer program. We shall usually show this colon in the following examples. You should remember that this is printed by the computer and so you don't need to type it when you copy these examples.

Here is a very simple program. Try it yourself.

```
: 9 =>
** 9
```

The first line is the program. The machine gives you the : prompt. You then type in 9 followed by the symbol => This symbol (typed using the = and > symbols with no spaces in between) is called the **printarrow**. It is part of POP-11's vocabulary and means 'print out the value of whatever is on its left'. At the end of a line you should hit the <RETURN> button on the right of your keyboard. The second line is the 'output'. POP-11 often prefaces its output with the symbol **. This is just to let you know that what follows is output.

Now, this definition of the printarrow seems a bit wordy, but you will see why we use this terminology if you try the following program:

```
: 8+4 =>
** 12
```

So, the printarrow really does print the *value* of whatever is to its left. This example also shows that POP-11 incorporates + as part of its vocabulary. Other simple arithmetic vocabulary includes - (minus), / (divided by) and * (multiply). Try some simple sums to convince yourself.

2.2 Words and lists

The kinds of programs written in POP-11 do not usually depend on numbers. In fact, there are two other very important kinds of objects in POP-11, these are words and lists. A word in POP-11 is quite similar to a word in English. A word is formed by surrounding several letters with double quotation marks. Try these programs

```
: "anteater" =>
** anteater
: "shop" =>
** shop
```

Note that the output from these programs does not show the quotation marks. This is just to save time. Also, words must not contain spaces. So "a cat" is not a word.

A good way to learn something about POP-11 is to make 'deliberate mistakes', this way you come to realize just what is and what is not possible in POP-11. Try the following:

```
: 9+"hercules" =>
MISHAP ...
```

The message following this MISHAP will tell you that you can't add a word and a number (which makes sense). Don't feel that it's wrong to get MISHAPs – they are very helpful and it's often useful just to experiment and discover what gives you MISHAPs and what doesn't.

Try the following

```
: 9+"seven" =>
MISHAP ..........
```

So, POP-11 won't allow you to add these two things. In fact the word
"seven" is not the same as the number 7 in POP-11. This illustrates the
fact that there are distinct kinds of objects in the POP-11 vocabulary,
these are called **datatypes**. In this example there is an object of the datatype **word** and an object of the datatype **number**. Numbers are always
represented as digits. If you look at the appropriate MISHAP message, you
will see that + only works for numbers.

A **list** is simply an ordered set of objects, often words. It is formed by
enclosing any number of objects (including none) with square brackets.
So that you don't get too bored with typing many sets of double quotation
marks, these are omitted for words in lists. It is assumed that an element
of a list is a word or a number unless you specify otherwise. The elements
of a list are separated by spaces. Try the following

```
: [once upon a time] =>
** [once upon a time]
```

Of course, the elements of a list don't have to form English phrases. For
example:

```
: [hill 3 apple axbyz 4] =>
** [hill 3 apple axbyz 4]
```

There are several things in POP-11's vocabulary specifically for dealing with lists. One is the concatenator <> (the 'less than' symbol followed
by the 'greater than' symbol, with no intervening spaces). This joins lists
together to form a bigger list. Try these:

```
: [once upon] <> [a time] =>
** [once upon a time]
: [shall I compare] <> [thee to a] <> [] <> [summers day] =>
** [shall I compare thee to a summers day]
```

Notice that you can join a list to another list which has nothing in it (called
the empty list). Of course, this doesn't affect the original list – you could
think of it as being like adding zero to a number, or multiplying it by one.

Another thing you can do with a list is to take its hd (head) and tl
(tail). hd and tl are examples of **procedures**. These procedures are
defined for you in the POP-11 system, they have a special meaning in
POP-11. In the next chapter you will see how to make your own procedures but for the time being you only need to know how to use these. hd
takes a list, and gives you the first element of that list – so, if the first
element of the list is a word, hd returns a word. tl takes a list and knocks

the first element off, giving you the rest of the list. Their format is as below, i.e. hd(LIST), tl(LIST). Try these

```
: hd([once upon a time]) =>
** once
: tl([The grand old Duke of York]) =>
** [grand old Duke of York]
```

Remember, the head of this list is a *word*, the tail of any list is a *list*.

To recap then, we have introduced numbers, some arithmetic operations, words, lists and some things you can do with them. Now, it is quite possible to combine many of these things. For example

```
: hd([8 10 12 14]) + 7 =>
** 15

: tl([once I loved]) <> [a pretty maid] =>
** [I loved a pretty maid]

: hd([jack jill bob]) <> [in the box] =>
MISHAP .................
```

To understand why the last example is not accepted by POP-11 you have to refer back to the meaning of <>. Remember, this joins lists together. But hd([jack jill bob]) is a *word* ("jack"), and so trying to use <> with it is doomed to failure. This is rather like trying to add a number to a word.

2.3 Variables

There is one last important type of entity in POP-11, which we have to look at before passing on to some more interesting examples. This is called a **variable**. A variable can be thought of as a place at which something else resides. One way to think of it is as a pigeon hole, called what the variable is called, and containing at most one thing (though this thing can be a word, number, list, or in fact many other things). As always, the best way to understand variables is to use them. So, try the following

```
: vars x;
: 23 -> x;
: x =>
** 23
```

There are several things to notice here. The first line says 'create a variable and call it x'. It could have been called any other group of letters we wanted (except a group which already has a meaning to the POP-11 system). This line ends in a semi-colon. In fact, all complete statements in POP-11 should be separated by a semi-colon, the previous examples do not show one because of the special nature of the printarrow at the end of each line. If in doubt, put one in.

The second line says 'assign the variable x the value 23' (or in the pigeon hole analogy 'put the number 23 in the variable x'). This is done using the **assignment arrow**, which is formed using the - (minus) and > (greater than) symbols with no intervening spaces.

The third line says 'print out the value of x' (i.e. what is in the variable). The fourth line gives us this value.

Now, here are some characteristics of a variable. A variable's name must start with a letter, but then can be any combination of letters or digits (with the exception that you cannot call a variable by a name which has a special meaning to the POP-11 system, e.g. hd or tl). A variable keeps its value until something else is assigned to it or until the end of your current POP-11 session – printing the value of the variable does not mean that you have de-assigned it. A variable is one of the most useful devices in many programming languages.

Here are some more examples of the use of variables. Comments are preceded by three semi-colons (this is the way to write comments in POP-11 – the system does not interpret as POP-11 anything to the right of three semi-colons on any particular line).

```
: vars a name friends;        ;;; make variables with these names
: "mike" -> name;             ;;; put the word "mike" in name

: [george edward charles] -> friends;
                              ;;; put this list in friends

: name =>
** mike
: friends =>
** [george edward charles]
: a =>
** <undef a>                  ;;; a doesn't contain anything yet

: hd(friends)                 ;;; we can use this variable to
** george                     ;;; avoid typing the whole lot

: hd(friends) -> name;        ;;; now we change the value of name
: name =>
** george

: tl(friends) -> friends;     ;;; we can replace the current value
: friends =>                  ;;; of friends with its own tail
** [edward charles]
```

Notice that when using a variable we just type its name. So,

```
: friends =>
** [edward charles]
```

really does mean print out the *value* of the variable to the left of the printarrow. Contrast this with typing

```
: "friends" =>
** friends
```

In this case the value of the first part of the statement is the word "friends". So, ordinarily, we distinguish between a variable and a word by the use of double quotation marks: if referring to a variable we do not enclose its name in double quotation marks.

Try the following

```
: neighbours =>
;;; DECLARING VARIABLE neighbours
** <undef neighbours>
```

The output shown here represents the POP-11 system's interpretation of your program. As the item to the left of the printarrow is not enclosed in double quotation marks, the system assumes that it is a variable. Furthermore, as you have not declared a variable called neighbours, the system does this for you; this is the meaning of the first output line. As you have not previously declared the variable, it clearly has no value yet. Hence the second line of output – variables are 'undefined' until they are assigned a value.

2.4 More lists, words and variables

We stated above that the elements of a list are assumed to be words or numbers, unless otherwise specified. Because of this, there is no need to put quotation marks around words in a list, they are understood to be there. This creates problems when we want to insert the value of variables into lists.

If you have not left the POP-11 system since the last set of examples, you will still have variables called name and friends, which have the values "george" and [edward charles] respectively. If you have not got these variables, create them for the following examples. Now try the following:

```
: [has anybody here seen name] =>
** [has anybody here seen name]
```

As each element in this list is understood to be between quotation marks, the POP-11 system treats them all as words, and simply prints them out in a list. In order to force an element of a list to be treated as a variable name, you need to precede it with a special symbol, the ^ character (called the 'hat'). Try this:

```
: [has anybody here seen ^name] =>
** [has anybody here seen george]
```

Of course, this syntax can be used inappropriately; for example,

```
: [has anybody here ^seen ^name] =>
;;; DECLARING VARIABLE seen
** [has anybody here <undef seen> george]
```

In this case the system treats seen as a variable, and as this is not a recognized variable name, the usual declaration is made for you, and the value of the variable remains undefined.

Now try the following:

```
: [I have friends called ^friends] =>
** [I have friends called [edward charles]]
```

The variable called friends has the value of a list and so this list is printed in the place of ^friends. Notice two things here: (i) that we have used a word called "friends" and a variable called friends; (ii) that it is quite permissible for an element of a list itself to be a list.

In fact there are cases when we might want to merge the contents of one list with another – that is to make each individual element of one list, an individual element of another. If we know that the value of a variable is a list, we can do this by preceding the variable name with the ^^ symbol ('double-hat'). For example,

```
: [I have friends called ^^friends] =>
** [I have friends called edward charles]
```

From the tools already available to us, we can make this sentence more tidy. For example,

```
: [I have friends called ^(hd(friends)) and ^^(tl(friends))] =>
** [I have friends called edward and charles]
```

Note that the above construction is possible because we know that friends is a two-element list. The hat symbol is used to evaluate the head, as the hd of this list is a word, the double-hat symbol is used to evaluate the tail, as the tl of this list is a one-element list. In cases where what is to be evaluated is complex (more than a simple variable name) the whole expression needs to be enclosed with round brackets.

You now know about some of the most fundamental elements of POP-11. We have met three different types of data, lists, words and numbers, and have come across variables and procedures. In the next chapter we shall introduce the idea of building new procedures of one's own. However, before going on to the next chapter you should read the following two brief sections. Section 2.5 introduces some other built-in facilities which you will come across as you progress through the rest of the book. A set of exercises follows (solutions are given in Appendix A). You will find it helpful to try the exercises provided at the end of each chapter. It is easy to read through examples of programming code without really understanding the structure of the code. The exercises will help you to test your own understanding.

2.5 Other useful built-in operations on lists

length: this procedure returns the length (number of elements) of a list. Hence:

```
: length([a b c]) =>
** 3
: length([a b [c d e] [f g] h]) =>
** 5
```

Notice the output from the second example here. The list has five elements, three words and two lists. The procedure length simply counts the number of elements in a list, regardless of whether these elements are words, lists, numbers or whatever.

rev: this procedure is used in exactly the same way as the other procedures (like hd, tl and length) and produces the given list with the order of its elements reversed. So,

```
: rev([one two three four]) =>
** [four three two one]

: rev([a b [c d e] [f g] h]) =>
** [h [f g] [c d e] b a]
```

oneof: this procedure returns one element of a given list at random. For example:

```
: oneof([a b [c d e] [f g] h]) =>
** b

: oneof([a b [c d e] [f g] h]) =>
** [f g]
```

Numbered access: When we want to discover the *n*th element of a list (called list, say) we can do so using the construction:

```
list(n)
```

Hence:

```
: friends(2) =>
** george
: [one two three four](3) =>
** three
```

This can sometimes be a simpler way of accessing lists than building complex combinations of hd and tl.

There are plenty of other built-in procedures for operating on lists in POP-11, but these are among the most important. If you want to follow up the other facilities you should look in your system documentation.

EXERCISES

You should try to answer these questions on paper, and then check them on your computer. What do the following print out?

2.1 hd([3]) =>

2.2 tl([3 4 5]) =>

2.3 hd([3 4 5]) =>

2.4 hd(tl([3 4 5])) =>

2.5 length(tl([3 4 5])) =>

2.6 What do the results of Exercises 2.4 and 2.5 tell you about the order in which POP-11 does its work when faced with complex expressions (i.e. expressions containing more than one instruction)?

What do the following print out?

2.7 vars weekdays;
      [mon tues wed thur fri] -> weekdays;
      [the days of the week are ^weekdays] =>
      length([the days of the week are ^^weekdays]) =>
      length([the days of the week are ^weekdays]) =>

2.8 Using the variable weekdays, write a list which prints as:
      ** [The days of the week are mon tues wed thur and fri]

Chapter 3 **Introduction to Procedures**

3.1 Elementary procedures

In POP-11 a procedure is a set of instructions which is given a name. The name is supplied by the user and follows the same rules as variable and word names (i.e. a set of alphanumerics, starting with a letter and containing no spaces). In most programs, procedures form the part which does the work, they are usually considered to be the elements of a large program.

Procedures are programs, they must first be defined and then used. Definitions may be typed directly onto the POP-11 system or stored in a file. Although you will want to use files quite soon, it is probably advisable to start off simply by typing procedure definitions directly. This way, your procedures will continue to exist until you leave the POP-11 system, but will then disappear.

Here is an example of a procedure definition:

```
: define proc1();
: [the cat sat on the mat] =>
: enddefine;
```

The first line tells the system to start the definition of a procedure called proc1. All lines that follow will be taken to be part of the procedure until you type enddefine. Notice then, that we have introduced two new 'reserved words', that is words which have a special meaning in POP-11, and so may not be used for other purposes. So, for example, you may not declare variables called define or enddefine. You will notice that this procedure name, proc1, is followed by empty round brackets. Some procedures take **arguments**, (i.e. extra information which the procedures use) and these arguments are placed in the round brackets. It is quite legitimate, however, to define procedures which take no arguments, and this is designated by leaving the brackets empty.

proc1 is a procedure which tells the system to print out the list [the cat sat on the mat]. You will notice, if you have typed the definition, that there has been no output. This is because there is a distinction between

24

defining and *executing* (using or 'calling') a procedure. The way to execute the procedure is simply to type its name, along with any necessary arguments. So, try this:

```
: proc1();
** [the cat sat on the mat]
```

Every time you type

```
: proc1();
```

this output will be delivered.

Procedures may be as long as you choose to make them, and may contain many sets of instructions. For example,

```
: define proc2();
: [one two three] =>
: [four] =>
: length([one two three four five]) =>
: enddefine;
:
: proc2();
** [one two three]
** [four]
** 5
```

Now we consider procedures which take arguments. Consider the following definition:

```
: define headtail(mylist);
: hd(mylist) =>
: tl(mylist) =>
: enddefine;
```

This procedure takes one argument, we have called it mylist. Arguments are treated as variables (as we shall shortly explain), and so may be called anything that a variable may be called.

In order to understand how this procedure works, we should first give examples of its use. Try these:

```
: headtail([one two three four]);
** one
** [two three four]
:
: headtail([the rain in spain]);
** the
** [rain in spain]
```

As with the examples of procedures with no arguments, the way to execute this procedure is to type its name. However, in this example the procedure needs to have some information on which to work. Let us follow through the operations involved in performing headtail on the list [one two three four].

The procedure definition includes an argument called mylist. This means that whenever the procedure headtail is executed, the argument that follows is called mylist. So, we may include operations on this variable in the body of the procedure definition, and the POP-11 system will actually perform these operations on whatever value mylist currently has. This means that we can write general purpose procedures which will perform the same set of operations on many different particular arguments. You can see from the two examples of execution that this procedure will work on any list. This property of procedures will prove to be very useful.

Although we have said that the procedure headtail is a general purpose procedure, one must still be careful only to provide arguments which will make sense to the body of the procedure. Try this execution of headtail:

```
: headtail("eric");
** MISHAP ...
```

The procedure fails to operate here because it is being asked to perform operations on a word, which only make sense when used on a list (i.e. hd and tl). Try to use the procedure on single element lists, and on empty lists. This will give you an insight into the nature of lists.

You should now realize that you have already been introduced to five procedures, all of them taking one argument. These are hd, tl, length, oneof and rev. These are all procedures which work on any list with which they are supplied as arguments. It is possible, then, to include procedures which are already defined, in the definition of other procedures. This is exactly what we have done in the definition of headtail.

Because of the limitation that procedure names may include no spaces, we sometimes make them easier to read by including underline dashes. An example may be the following procedure definition:

```
: define first_last(alist);
: hd(alist) =>
: hd(rev(alist)) =>
: enddefine;
```

What do you think this procedure does?

Of course you may call procedures by any number of obscure names, but in order to keep a track of what procedures do, we usually try to give them a name which makes sense. You will be surprised how quickly you forget what procedures called 'rhgf' or 'jagger' do.

3.2 The stack: the end of deception

We now have to confess that we have not given you the whole truth. In order to simplify our explanations we have given a rather trivial definition of certain ideas in POP-11, notably the printarrow. In fact, the printarrow has two different meanings, one when used inside a procedure, and one when used outside (i.e. when typed directly to the POP-11 system). In order to understand both of these uses, we need to examine an entity called the **stack**.

The stack can be thought of as a place where objects are kept until we need them. Every time a new object is put on the stack, the objects already on it are pushed down a position – rather like putting plates on a cafe plate-stack. This means that when we take something off the stack, it is usually the case that the last object put on, is the first object taken off.

Now, why is this relevant? To answer this we have to think about how elements are put onto the stack. The way to put an entity onto the stack is simply to type it (or its name, in the case of variables) into the POP-11 system. Try the following:

```
: vars mylist;           ;;; declare a variable and assign
: [a b c] -> mylist;     ;;; it the value of this list

: mylist;                ;;; put mylist on the stack
: [size 12];             ;;; put this list on the stack
: 3; 4; 5;               ;;; put these numbers on the stack
```

So far there has been no output. If we now type the printarrow, the following result is obtained:

```
: =>
** [a b c] [size 12] 3 4 5
```

What the printarrow actually does when used in this fashion (that is, when used outside a procedure) is to print the value of *everything* on the stack. In this case, the order of printing is the same as the the order in which the the elements were put on the stack. As each element is printed, it is removed from the stack.

It is often the case that the stack is empty, i.e. if we typed the printarrow again now, we should see that there is nothing left on the stack. We can now make sense of the earlier use of the printarrow. If we type

```
: [a b c d e] =>
** [a b c d e]
```

what this means to the POP-11 system is: (i) leave the list [a b c d e] on the stack; (ii) print off the value of all the elements of the stack. If the stack was previously empty, this gives the impression that the purpose of the printarrow is simply to print the value of whatever is to its left.

The assignment arrow also works using the stack. However, in this case the arrow takes the value of the top entity only, removes it from the stack, and assigns this to the variable on its right. So:

```
: [home sweet home] -> myvariable;
```

has exactly the same meaning as:

```
: [home sweet home];
:
: -> myvariable;
```

Consider the following example:

```
: [a b c];
: 3;
: [London Paris Munich] -> myvariable;
```

What will be printed out when we type myvariable =>? Try it:

```
: myvariable =>
** [a b c]   3   [London Paris Munich]
```

To understand why this occurs, think about what happens during the various stages of the program. Table 3.1 shows the various states of the stack during the process of running this example. You will see from the final stages shown in the table that once the stack is cleared, we can go back to our original conception of the printarrow.

The second meaning of the printarrow, when used inside a procedure, is simpler. In this case the printarrow simply takes the value of the *top* element of the stack, removes it, and prints it. So, using the procedure proc1, as defined in Section 3.1, we can see how this usage works in the following example:

```
: [a b c];
: 3;
: proc1();
** [the cat sat on the mat]
```

As the printarrow used here is embedded inside proc1, only the top of the stack (i.e. the list put on the stack immediately before the printarrow is used) is printed.

Finally, you should know that there are occasions when we lose track of the contents of the stack. On these occasions, an interrupt command will completely clear the stack without printing out its contents. When this is done, the message:

```
Setpop
:
```

appears on your screen. Interrupt commands are specific to computers, and so you will need to find out just what the command is on your

Table 3.1 Various states of the stack at different stages of running the program.

Stage	Input	Stack
1	[a b c];	[a b c]
2	3;	3 [a b c]
3	[London Paris Munich]	[London Paris Munich] 3 [a b c]
4	-> myvariable;	3 [a b c]
5	myvariable	[London Paris Munich] 3 [a b c]
6	=>	OUTPUT: [a b c] 3 [London Paris Munich] STACK EMPTY
7	myvariable	[London Paris Munich]
8	=>	OUTPUT: [London Paris Munich] STACK EMPTY

computer. A common one is <CTRL C> (hold down the control button on your terminal and press the C key), though you should check with your computer operators before using it. You should not need to use this device yet, though you will probably need to know about it as you progress through the course.

3.3 Using the stack for communication

Each of the procedures defined in Section 3.1 prints out a result every time the procedure is executed. They all have printarrows included in the procedure definition. Here is another such procedure, though this one does some simple arithmetic:

```
: define double(num);
: num+num =>
: enddefine;

: double(3);
** 6
```

This procedure simply prints double the value of any numerical argument with which it is provided. Now, there is a different way of defining this procedure, such that the result is not simply printed on every execution. This is:

```
: define double(num);
: num+num
: enddefine;
```

This procedure leaves its result on the stack – to find out the value of what the procedure leaves on the stack, it must be explicitly printed after each execution:

```
: double(5) =>
** 10
```

Whether the printarrow appears inside the procedure definition or not is not just a matter of whim. In fact the second procedure definition is much more flexible that the first, in that we can now do more things with the result than simply print it out. For example, we could assign it to a variable, thus:

```
: vars newnum;
: double(6) -> newnum;
```

Our variable newnum now has the value 12. We may want to use this variable again. For example,

```
: double(newnum) =>
** 24
```

So, leaving a value on the stack gives us more flexibility than simply printing it off each time the procedure is called. This style also allows us to use the following construction:

```
: double(double(4)) =>
** 16
```

When POP-11 encounters such a construction it first evaluates the inner-most procedure, in this case double(4) which returns the value 8. If there is no printarrow included in the definition, then 8 is left on the stack and this is picked up as an argument to the second procedure – in this case double again. Had we included the printarrow in the procedure definition, the above construction would not be possible, as the first call of double would have given a result (of 8) which would have been removed from the stack and printed. This would have left no value for the second (outer) call of double to work on. Hence the construction would not succeed.

You should notice that the procedures introduced in Chapter 2, hd, tl, rev, length, etc., are all of the type which leave their results on the stack. Hence it is permissible to assign their results to variables, or to combine them in complex constructions such as that given above. In fact, most procedures are defined in this way. It is therefore a good idea to get into the habit of defining procedures which leave results on the stack. More complex programs are often built out of several procedures and the stack provides a convenient way of communicating between these procedures. Most of the examples which follow depend on procedure communication through the stack.

3.4 Procedures with several arguments

There is no limit to the number of arguments which may be provided to a procedure. When there are more than one, these are separated by commas in both definition and execution. So, try the following procedure definition:

```
: define join_ends(list1,list2);
: tl(list1) <> tl(list2)
: enddefine;
```

This procedure simply returns a list comprising the tails of two lists, for example:

```
: join_ends([a b c],[d e f]) =>
** [b c e f]
```

Notice that we can use variable names as arguments for executing procedures instead of typing out the whole list each time we call the procedure. Let us create three variables for use in these examples:

```
: vars v1 v2 v3;
: [a b c] -> v1;
: [one two three four] -> v2;
: [doh ray me] -> v3;
```

So,

```
: join_ends(v2,v1) =>
** [two three four b c]
```

A three variable procedure definition might look like this:

```
: define odd_join(list1,list2,list3);
: list1 <> rev(list2) <> list3
: enddefine;
```

So,

```
: odd_join(v1,v2,v3) =>
** [a b c four three two one doh ray me]
```

and

```
: odd_join(v2,v1,v3) =>
** [one two three four c b a doh ray me]
```

The rule in executing procedures is that they must be typed in the form in which they are defined – i.e. if the definition contains *n* arguments, the execution must contain *n* arguments. Hence:

```
: odd_join(v2,v1) =>
```

will produce a MISHAP message.

3.5 Local and global variables

Each variable has a **scope**, that is a set of circumstances under which it may be used. The scope of a variable depends on where you choose to declare it. Variables which are declared outside procedures (as with all those we have considered so far) can be used under any circumstances until you log out of the POP-11 system. These are called **global** variables. However, sometimes we only need to use a variable for a limited purpose, e.g. for the lifetime of a procedure execution. In these cases we make a declaration *inside* the procedure, and the variable may only be used inside that procedure. These variables are called **local** variables. (In fact the scope of a local variable is that procedure in which it is declared, and any procedures which are called as a result of that execution. However, use of this extended scope can lead to messy programs and so we will avoid giving examples dependent on this fact. It is almost always neater to communicate through the stack or through global variables.) Consider the following example procedure definition:

```
: define all_but_last(list);
: vars temp;
: rev(list) -> temp;
: tl(temp) -> temp;
: rev(temp)
: enddefine;
```

In this procedure we have declared a local variable called temp. On the third line the list provided as an argument is operated on by the procedure rev and the result is assigned to temp. In the fourth line the tail of temp is now assigned to temp (remember that we can update variables in this fashion, see page 19). Finally, the procedure rev is applied to the current value of temp. Hence we have:

```
: all_but_last([red green yellow blue]) =>
** [red green yellow]
```

In the execution of this example the variable temp successively has values:

Step 1. [blue yellow green red]

Step 2. [yellow green red]

and it is the reverse of this list which is left on the stack. However, once the procedure is executed, the variable ceases to exist. If you now try to discover the value of temp, you will find that it is undefined. So the variable temp is *local* to this procedure.

Of course we could have defined the above procedure like this:

```
: define all_but_last(list);
: rev(tl(rev(list)))
: enddefine;
```

However, it is good practice to make procedures as readable as possible. You should agree that the second definition of this procedure is rather opaque. The use of local variables can make procedures more transparent. There are, in fact, further uses for local variables which will be introduced in the next chapter.

As an example of the use of both local and global variables in a procedure, consider the following:

```
: vars myvar;
: define first_two(sentence);
: vars lvar;
: [^(sentence(1))] -> myvar;
: [^(sentence(2))] -> lvar;
: myvar <> lvar
: enddefine;
```

If we executed this procedure thus:

```
: first_two([once upon a time]) =>
** [once upon]
```

we could now examine the value of myvar, as it is a global variable:

```
: myvar =>
** [once]
```

However, the local variable, lvar, has ceased to exist:

```
: lvar =>
;;; DECLARING VARIABLE lvar
** <undef lvar>
```

As the system does not know of the global variable lvar, it creates one when you ask for a value as above. This means that we have a local and a global variable, each with the same name. In these cases a variable used inside a procedure body always assumes the value of the local variable. However, you should avoid this situation altogether if you can – two variables called the same thing can soon lead to confusion.

Consideration of the scope of variables should bring you to some further understanding of procedure arguments. An argument for a procedure is really just a variable local to that procedure. This is why we can use the same names as arguments for several procedures without them interfering with each other. Having said this, it is a good idea to avoid using the same names for procedure arguments. Again, good programmers make their programs as readable as possible. A program containing many different entities all with the same name will present unnecessary difficulties for a reader.

EXERCISES

Write procedures which print the following:

3.1 The last two elements of a given list.

3.2 The last element of a given list – but don't use rev. (Hint: think about how you could use length.)

3.3 The product and mean of three numbers.

Chapter 4 **Control Structures and more Procedures**

4.1 A note about files and editors

Before we go on to discuss the nature of POP-11 control structures, it is a good idea to consider the use of files. So far we have recommended that you type procedure definitions directly to the POP-11 system. This has two disadvantages: (i) any errors made in the definition (e.g. typing errors) mean that you have to re-type the whole procedure; and (ii) procedures defined in this way will disappear when you finish the current session of POP-11. In order to overcome these shortcomings, you should now investigate the use of files.

To create a file you need an editor. This will also allow you to make changes to your files. The editor which comes with POPLOG is called VED, and you will probably want to use this. However, the way you use this editor will vary according to the type of terminal you use, and according to certain decisions made by your local computer operators. You should read your local documentation on VED and familiarize yourself with the use of this editor. Once you have created files, you will be able to use them whenever you wish, e.g. in successive POP-11 sessions.

In order to make procedures defined in files available to your current POP-11 session, you need to use the `load` command, that is,

```
: load FILENAME;
```

where `FILENAME` is the name of your file. Once a file is loaded, all procedures in it will be available for use.

As the example procedures which follow are longer than those in Chapter 3, we strongly recommend that you put all these into files. You are very likely to make errors in your definitions and it is annoying to have to re-type the whole procedure every time you start a new POP-11 session. In order to reinforce this, we shall now stop providing the colon prompt to the left of procedure definitions. However, we will give the prompt whenever we mean to designate input directly to the POP-11 system.

4.2 Conditionals – the `if` statement

Like many other procedural languages, POP-11 has a built-in conditional facility. The format of the `if` statement is:

35

```
if CONDITION
then ACTION 1
else ACTION 2
endif;
```

This should be read as meaning: if CONDITION is true, then do ACTION 1, else (i.e. if CONDITION is false) do ACTION 2, endif (end conditional statement). A simple POP-11 procedure will illustrate this:

```
define size(num);
if num > 1000
then [its a biggy]
else [small number]
endif
enddefine;
```

This procedure takes one argument, this has to be a number as the operator > (greater than) is used on it. size will return the list [its a biggy] if the argument is larger than 1000, and [small number] if it is not. Hence:

```
: size(2001) =>
** [its a biggy]
: size(32) =>
** [small number]
```

The second line of this procedure says: if the statement num > 1000 leaves the value <true> on the stack.... You can see this by typing:

```
: 1003 > 1000 =>
** <true>
: 32 > 1000 =>
** <false>
```

Such comparisons as < and > are actually special kinds of procedures which have been designed to leave <true> or <false> on the stack. You can see this with other such procedures (or 'operators' as they are called):

```
: 3+4 = 7 =>
** <true>
: 3+4 = 34 =>
** <false>
```

However, this need not concern us unduly, and it is easier to pronounce the second line of the program: 'if num is larger than 1000...'.

Here is a procedure which takes two arguments, a list and a number. The procedure produces the anum-th element of the list, but only if the list has at least anum elements. This way we can avoid asking the system to do anything which is impossible, and hence avoid MISHAPs.

```
define nth(alist,anum);
if length(alist) < anum
then [list not long enough]
else alist(anum)
endif
enddefine;
```

So,

```
: nth([the capital of Canada is Ottawa],4) =>
** Canada
: nth([Doh ray me],6) =>
** [list not long enough]
```

As with the operators > and = we can arrange to make our procedures return <true> or <false>. Thus:

```
define islong(list);
if length(list) > 7
then true
else false
endif
enddefine;
```

```
: islong([the capital of Canada is Ottawa though it is small]) =>
** <true>
: islong([a little list]) =>
** <false>
```

So, to make a procedure return <true> or <false>, we simply write true or false in the ACTION parts of the procedure. When printed these values are enclosed in angle brackets. (Can you think of a very short definition of islong?)

We can now use these 'true or false' procedures as conditions for other procedures. Consider the conditional print procedure:

```
define print_short(sentence);
if islong(sentence)
then [cant be bothered to print all that] =>
else sentence =>
endif
enddefine;
```

The conditional statement can be extended beyond this simple use by employing the elseif construction. Use of elseif has the following format:

```
if  CONDITION 1
then  ACTION 1
elseif  CONDITION 2
then  ACTION 2
elseif  CONDITION 3
then  ACTION 3
else  ACTION 4
endif;
```

In the execution of such a statement there are several possible ACTIONs (four here). However, you should note that only *one* ACTION is ever performed. If CONDITION 1 is true, then ACTION 1 is performed and the POP-11 system jumps directly to the endif statement – even if a subsequent CONDITION is also true. The aim of the POP-11 system is to find the first CONDITION which is true, perform the corresponding ACTION and leave the conditional construction. Because of this, the ACTION following the else statement (penultimate line) is referred to as the **default**, i.e. it is only performed if none of the above CONDITIONs is true.

The procedure below takes a *word* as its only argument.

```
define capital(country);
if country = "England"
then [the capital of England is London]
elseif country = "USA"
then [the capital of USA is Washington]
elseif country = "Australia"
then [the capital of Australia is Canberra]
else [I dont know the capital of ^country]
endif
enddefine;
```

You may continue to expand this program to be as long as you wish, simply by adding more conditionals. Furthermore, the ACTION parts of such a program may include more than one action. If this is the case, these are separated by semi-colons. Here's an example:

```
define middle(list);
vars listlen mid;
length(list) -> listlen;
if listlen > 2
then tl(list) -> mid;
     rev(mid) -> mid;
     tl(mid) -> mid;
     rev(mid) -> mid;
     mid
else [list not long enough]
endif
enddefine;
```

This is rather a clumsy definition of middle, though you should experiment with it to establish exactly what it does.

4.3 Recursion using conditionals

The idea of **recursion** is a powerful one which you will need to use as you begin to construct your own models. Recursive procedures in POP-11 are those which call themselves – that is, there is a call of the procedure inside the procedure body. This is useful in a number of circumstances, particularly when we are operating on lists whose lengths we do not know.

Consider a solution to the following problem. Write a procedure which, given a list of numbers, returns a list containing the doubles of all these numbers. In the solution we have to perform the doubling on each of the numbers encountered in turn. We will build this procedure up part by part.

First consider a procedure which just prints out the double of each number of a list of numbers:

```
define double_all(listnums);
hd(listnums)*2 =>
double_all(tl(listnums))
enddefine;
```

What does this procedure do? First of all it prints out the double of the value of the head of listnums. Next it performs double_all on the tail of listnums. So, the next thing to be printed out is the double of the head of tl(listnums), i.e. the second element of the original listnums. Next it tries to perform double_all on the tail of the new value of listnums and so on. Let us try to execute this procedure:

```
: double_all([1 2 3 4]);
** 2
** 4
** 6
** 8
MISHAP ...
```

Why have we got a MISHAP message here? The answer is that we have failed to include a **stopping condition** in the procedure definition. The last successful call of double_all is made on the list [4]. The head of this list, 4, is doubled and printed. The procedure then tries to apply double_all to the tail of this list. Now the tail of [4] is [], the empty list. The first thing that double_all([]) tries to do is to print double the value of the head of this list. However, hd([]) causes a MISHAP, as there is no head to this list. Hence the MISHAP when we tried to execute the procedure.

There is a very useful device in POP-11 called `trace`. The trace facility allows you to observe what is going on inside a procedure at successive moments of its execution. In order to trace a procedure we simply type

```
: trace PROCEDURE_NAME;
```

So, let's try this with `double_all`:

```
: trace double_all;
```

Now we execute the procedure again, and observe what happens:

```
: double_all([1 2 3 4]);

>double_all [1 2 3 4]
** 2
!>double_all [2 3 4]
** 4
!!>double_all [3 4]
** 6
!!!>double_all [4]
** 8
!!!!>double_all []

;;; MISHAP ...

Setpop
:
```

You can follow this output through, observing what the procedure is trying to operate on at each successive call. We can see from this output that the procedure has failed when it is trying to do `double_all([])`.

What all this has told us is that we need to tell the procedure what to do when it is faced with an empty list. We can do this by editing the procedure into the following form:

```
define double_all(listnums);
if listnums = []
then
else hd(listnums)*2 =>
     double_all(tl(listnums))
endif
enddefine;
```

This new procedure says, `if` the list is empty, `then` do nothing. If the list is not empty, then print out double its head, and do `double_all` on its tail. You will see then that lines 2 and 3 represent a stopping condition; once the list is empty, nothing else happens. Try the new procedure:

```
: double_all([1 2 3 4]);

>double_all [1 2 3 4]
** 2
!>double_all [2 3 4]
** 4
!!>double_all [3 4]
** 6
!!!>double_all [4]
** 8
!!!!>double_all []
!!!!<double_all
!!!<double_all
!!<double_all
!<double_all
<double_all
:
```

Notice that on a successfully called procedure, the trace facility notes both entry to and exit from procedure calls.

We can now remove the tracing as follows:

```
: untrace double_all;
```

The trace facility is a useful **debugging aid**, it helps us to find errors in procedures. However, there is no need to follow through the workings of the procedure once it is behaving as we wish. So,

```
: double_all([5 4 3 2 1]);
** 10
** 8
** 6
** 4
** 2
```

We have not finished with this procedure yet. Remember that we specified that the procedure should return a list of all the doubles of an original list. This procedure simply returns each double separately. We can fix this with the following edited version

```
define double_all(listnums);
if listnums = []
then []
else [^(hd(listnums)*2)] <> double_all(tl(listnums))
endif
enddefine;
```

Look at the fourth line initially. This line says: take the head of the list, multiply it by two, and put that result in a list. Next, join this list onto the result of doing double_all on the tail of the initial list. In order for this to work, the result of doing double_all must always be a list (as <> only works on lists). Now, we know that double_all usually returns a list (as on the fourth line). However, we must now ensure that the result of doing double_all([]) is also a list. To do this we simply say that double_all([]) should return the value []. Now we have a complete procedure which leaves its result on the stack. For example,

```
: double_all([2 4 6 8 10]) =>
** [4 8 12 16 20]
```

Recursion is not only useful for operating on every member of a list. Instead we could just check each number of a list until we are satisfied that some relation holds. Consider, for example, a procedure called ismember which returns <true> if a given element is in a given list, and <false> if it is not. A 'wordy' definition of this procedure might be:

Check the element against the head of the list. If these two things are the same, then return <true> and don't bother looking any further. If these two are not the same then go through the procedure again, this time using the tail of the list. If you go through the whole list and still have not found a match for the element, then return <false>.

Such a procedure is defined below:

```
define ismember(element,list);
if list = []
then false
elseif element = hd(list)
then true
else ismember(element,tl(list))
endif
enddefine;
```

Use the procedure on a few example arguments. Before you execute it on the machine, take a piece of paper and go through the program step by step with some example arguments. You should try to understand exactly how this procedure works.

In more complex situations than those shown here, whole programs can behave recursively. Consider, for example, the problem of searching through a complicated network like the London Underground in order to find a route between two stations. You might plausibly want to start at a given station and then try the next station on a line until you either hit the destination or the terminus. If you hit the end of the line you might want to 'back-up' to try other lines in the same fashion and so on. Such problems as this, common in AI, are very well suited to recursive solutions. We will return to the technique and its possible applications in the later chapters when we discuss writing AI programs. In the meantime, the following sections provide some alternatives to this technique and introduce some powerful control structures.

4.4 The until construction: iteration

The until construction in POP-11 has the following format:

```
until CONDITION
do ACTION
enduntil;
```

This should be read as saying: until CONDITION is true, do ACTION, enduntil (stop until process).

This construction is known as a **loop** conditional. On encountering such a construction, POP-11 first checks to see whether CONDITION is true, if it is then the system ignores ACTION and jumps to enduntil. If CONDITION is false, then ACTION is performed, the system returns to the CONDITION line, and checks to see whether it is now true. The whole process then begins again. The same rules for ACTION hold in until loops as hold in if statements, i.e. ACTION can comprise many actions, and these are separated by semi-colons. In fact there is almost always more than one action in the ACTION part of this construction.

As an example, consider the procedure double_all as written in until format:

```
define double_all2(listn);
until listn = []
do  hd(listn)*2 =>
    tl(listn) -> listn
enduntil
enddefine;
```

So, the until conditional requires us to specify a stopping condition. If you try this procedure you will notice that it does not return the required value (a list), but once again prints items out separately. In fact, we can enclose a *whole structure* in a list. This way the results of that structure are placed in the list. Here is an example:

```
define double_all2(listn);
[^(
until listn = []
do  hd(listn)*2;
    tl(listn) -> listn
enduntil
)]
enddefine;
```

Hence,

```
: double_all2([3 5 7 9]) =>
** [6 10 14 18]
```

However, this is not the easiest way to follow what is going on in the procedure. A more verbose, but easier definition would be the following:

```
define double_all2(listn);
vars temp;
[] -> temp;
until listn = []
do   temp <> [^(hd(listn)*2)] -> temp;
     tl(listn) -> listn
enduntil;
temp
enddefine;
```

Here we have used a temporary store (the local variable called temp), and updated it for each new element of the list. The final value of temp is left on the stack in the penultimate line of the procedure. Notice that we had to initialize temp to a sensible value – in this case []. Here, we need temp to start life as a list in order that the <> operator can sensibly be applied to it on the first run through the loop.

This technique of looping through a set of instructions, continually changing the state of certain variables, and checking each time to see whether a condition has been met, is called **iteration**. Between them, recursion and iteration make up the most useful techniques in many programming languages. However, many programming languages only have the facilities for one of these techniques and it is a strong argument in favour of POP-11 that it has both.

Now we'll look at some more iterative procedures:

```
define all_squares();
vars i;
0 -> i;
until i = 20
do   i*i =>
     i+1 -> i
enduntil
enddefine;
```

Here is a procedure which takes no arguments, and prints out the squares of all the numbers up to, and including 19. Notice that this procedure does not print the square of 20. As soon as i = 20, the until loop stops. So if you wanted the squares of numbers up to 20, you would need to say

```
until i = 21
```

Now consider this procedure:

```
define all_squares(num);
vars i;
0 -> i;
until i = num
do  i*i =>
    i+1 -> i
enduntil
enddefine;
```

This procedure prints out all the squares of the numbers up to (but not including) the argument provided. So,

```
: all_squares(5);
** 0
** 1
** 4
** 9
** 16
```

Now try this:

```
: all_squares(5.5);
** 0
** 1
** 4
** 9
** 16
** 25
** 36
** 49
   .
   .
   .
MISHAP
```

What has happened here? This is a good way to make yourself unpopular with other people using the system. The procedure just keeps going until the numbers it is trying to generate are too big for the particular computer you are using. This is because the stopping condition is never reached! i is never equal to 5.5 and cannot ever be. This is because i starts life as a whole number (0) and is always updated by 1. So i can never have any value which is not a whole number. This is a classic pitfall for iterative procedures. To get round it you need to ensure that your stopping condition is general enough to cover all eventualities. One way would be to substitute for the line

```
until i = num
```

the line

```
until i > num
```

This way you will never cause the procedure to go sailing past the condition, as long as it is provided with a number. Just how rigorous you make your stopping condition of course depends on the kind of input which your procedure is likely to get. There is a pay-off here between making your procedures as robust (difficult to abuse) as possible, and the time and effort spent in writing them. These decisions have to be made by the programmer.

Now let's have a look at some procedures iterating on lists of words. We could, for instance, define our own version of the existing procedure rev. We'll call it reverse as rev is a reserved word:

```
define reverse(list);
vars result;
[] -> result;
until list = []
do  [^(hd(list))] <> result -> result;
    tl(list) -> list
enduntil;
result
enddefine;
```

If you still have the procedure ismember as defined in the last section, we could use it to write a procedure which returns an element common to two lists:

```
define isinboth(list1,list2);
vars result;
[no common word] -> result;
until list1 = []
do  if ismember(hd(list1),list2)
    then hd(list1) -> result
    else
    endif;
    tl(list1) -> list1
enduntil;
result
enddefine;
```

In this procedure, we have combined the use of until and if statements – this is a legitimate thing to do. However, the procedure is quite complex, and furthermore, there is an assumption built-in that there is only one element common to both lists. If there is more than one, the procedure returns the latest common element to appear in list1. Try this out by supplying the procedure with various arguments.

There are, of course, many ways of writing procedures to do the same job. For example, a more elegant definition of isinboth, this time one which returns the first element of list1 to appear in list2, would be purely recursive. For example,

```
define isinboth(list1,list2);
if list1 = []
then [no common word]
elseif ismember(hd(list1),list2)
then hd(list1)
else isinboth(tl(list1),list2)
endif
enddefine;
```

A common response which students make on being shown such a procedure is: 'Yes, I can understand how the procedure works, but I could not have written it from scratch'. The only answer to this is that you *will* learn by experience. There are no hard and fast rules about how to construct the most elegant solution to a given problem, one simply becomes adept at spotting different solutions. Try to construct your own example problems and solve them using both recursive and iterative techniques. You will soon find that some of your procedures are unwieldy and difficult to read, while others appear quite neat. As with all skills, practice makes better.

4.5 Other control structures

In addition to the until construction, POP-11 provides three further important looping constructions, while, repeat and for. These are very similar to the until construction, with the exception that their stopping conditions take a different form. We will consider the while loop first.

The while construction has the following format:

```
while CONDITION
do ACTION
endwhile;
```

This should be read as saying: while CONDITION is true, do ACTION, endwhile (end while loop). So, in this case, ACTION is performed whenever CONDITION is true. This is really the negation of the until loop, in which ACTION is performed as long as CONDITION is false. Consider the following redefinition of all_squares:

```
define all_squares(num);
vars i;
0 -> i;
while i < num
do  i*i =>
    i+1 -> i
endwhile
enddefine;
```

So,

```
while i < num
```

has been used instead of

```
until i > num
```

Which construction you choose to use depends on your preference, and the degree of elegance of the resulting definition. In fact the two uses are slightly different in effect – can you spot how? (Hint: when does each stop?)

In fact there is a built-in procedure in POP-11 called not. This procedure takes one argument, and returns <false> if the argument is true, and <true> if the argument is false. Hence

```
until CONDITION
```

is exactly equivalent to

```
while not(CONDITION)
```

This gives you the answer to the question posed above: 'less than' is not the same as 'not bigger than'.

The next iterative construction which we will consider is used only when one wants to perform actions on each element of a list. It is called a for loop and has the following format:

```
for VARIABLE in LIST
do ACTION
endfor;
```

In this case, VARIABLE is a variable name which successively takes on the value of each element of the list LIST. Here is an example use of a for loop:

```
: vars x;
: for x in [1 2 3]
: do x*2 =>
: endfor;
```

```
** 2
** 4
** 6
```

So, on each loop x takes the value of the next list element. The construction terminates automatically when it reaches the end of the list.

Commonly for loops are used as alternatives to until loops when iterating through lists. As an example, look back at the definition of reverse on page 46. This procedure could equally well have been written:

```
define reverse(list);
vars result element;
[] -> result;
for element in list
do [^element] <> result -> result
endfor;
result
enddefine;
```

The final looping construction which we will consider here is repeat. This is perhaps the simplest loop of all and its format is as follows:

```
repeat NUMBER times
ACTION
endrepeat;
```

In this construction, NUMBER can be any positive integer, and ACTION can contain several actions, separated by semi-colons. A simple procedure definition might be:

```
define print3(list);
repeat 3 times
list =>
endrepeat
enddefine;

: print3([hip hip hooray]);
** [hip hip hooray]
** [hip hip hooray]
** [hip hip hooray]
```

The disadvantage of the repeat construction is that one needs to specify how many loops through ACTION are to be performed, rather than imposing some general criterion for stopping. However, if we want to write procedures which work on different lengths of list, we could use variables to make the construction more general. For example,

```
define double_all(list);
vars listlen;
```

```
length(list) -> listlen;
repeat listlen times
   hd(list)*2 =>
   tl(list) -> list
endrepeat
enddefine;
```

4.6 Some rules for semi-colons

We have been very vague about the use of semi-colons in POP-11 so far. The rules for their use are rather complicated and we have postponed a formal explanation until you have seen quite a few examples of POP-11 code. In order to understand the use of semi-colons you need to understand what constitutes a **statement**.

A statement in POP-11 is any complete construction. A variable assignment is a statement; so is a value put on the stack. Furthermore, procedure definitions and conditional constructions are statements. The general rule is: statements are separated by semi-colons. Consider the following example:

```
: vars name;
: "mike" -> name;
```

These two statements are followed by semi-colons in order to tell the POP-11 system that they are different statements from the ones that follow.

Now, a procedure definition is always followed by a semi-colon, in order to tell the system that this constitutes a complete statement. However, the procedure definition syntax is set up to expect the following form:

```
define proc(args);
STATEMENT
enddefine;
```

If there is only one statement inside a procedure body it does not need to be followed by a semi-colon. However, if there are many statements, these need to be separated by semi-colons, for example,

```
define proc(args);
STATEMENT 1;
STATEMENT 2;
STATEMENT 3
enddefine;
```

Note that the last statement does not need a semi-colon.

Conditional structures are themselves complete statements. Consider the if construction. This is set up to expect the following pattern:

```
if ONE STATEMENT ONLY
then ANY NUMBER OF STATEMENTS
else ANY NUMBER OF STATEMENTS
endif;
```

In the lines following then and else we may legally insert several statements. Once again, these must be separated by semi-colons, though the last statement need not be followed by a semi-colon. The same rules apply to the do ACTION section of all the structures we have considered in this chapter.

One final nuisance rule applies here. This is that the printarrow, =>, has its own built-in semi-colon. You never need to follow the printarrow with a semi-colon. It is not important that you know why this is the case, but if you go back to the discussion of the stack in Chapter 3, you may begin to understand why this makes sense.

You may like to re-read some of the example procedures provided so far and examine them for use of semi-colons. As an exercise, try to re-write the procedures yourself after memorizing their functions and then check your use of semi-colons with the given procedures.

4.7 Output locals

In some of the procedures defined earlier in this chapter, a local variable is declared in the first line of the procedure body. This variable is then operated on in some way, and its value is left on the stack in the final line of the procedure body (see, for example, the second definition of double_all2, or the first definition of isinboth). There is a syntactic device in POP-11 which allows you to do exactly this, but with rather less effort. This device is known as use of **output locals**.

Here is the format of the standard device:

```
define proc(args);
vars temp;
  .
  .
  .
temp
enddefine;
```

(We have called the local variable temp, though of course you may give it any legal variable name.)

Exactly the same effect is achieved with the following format:

```
define proc(args) -> temp;
    .
    .
    .
enddefine;
```

In this second format, temp is considered a local variable all the way through the procedure, though you do not have to include a variable declaration in the definition. Furthermore, the value of temp is automatically left on the stack at the end of the procedure execution. In this format, the variable temp is known as an output local.

We find that this construction tends to confuse students, and it does not actually save very much time or effort. For these reasons we shall mostly avoid output locals in our examples throughout the rest of this book. However, you will see them used in other people's programs, and so you need to know just what they mean. Of course, you are free to use output locals yourself if you find the syntax straightforward.

EXERCISES

Write procedures which perform the following tasks. If the solution entails either recursion or iteration, write procedures in both forms.

4.1 Given a list of countries, the procedure will apply the procedure capital (defined in Section 4.2) to each element.

4.2 Given a list and an element, the procedure will tell you how many times the element appears in the list.

4.3 Given two lists, the procedure will return *all* the elements common to both.

4.4 Given a list of numbers, the procedure will give you their sum total.

4.5 Expand Exercise 4.4 so that the procedure gives you pretty output containing a summary of the numbers in a given list (e.g. the number of numbers, their total, range and mean).

Chapter 5 **Pattern Matching and the Database**

In this chapter we begin to get down to some procedures which will be used extensively in AI-type programs. The use of matching facilities and the database can lead to some powerful programs without recourse to an opaque style. The knowledge you have collected so far, taken in conjunction with this chapter, will enable you to write programs which a few years ago were the exclusive province of computer experts.

5.1 The **matches** operator

5.1.1 Simple matching

We have already met some arithmetic operators, for example <, > and =. We will now introduce a further operator for use with lists. This is called matches. The operator returns <true> if the list to its left matches the list to its right, and <false> if it does not. The simplest form of matching occurs when the two lists are equivalent. Hence:

```
: [my fair lady] matches [my fair lady] =>
** <true>
: [my fair lady] matches [pygmalion] =>
** <false>
```

Of course we can use the hat and double-hat signs to evaluate variables in these lists in the normal way. So,

```
: vars family examples;
: "cat" -> family;
: [lion tiger and puma] -> examples;
:
: [Examples of the cat are lion tiger and puma]
: matches [Examples of the ^family are ^^examples] =>
** <true>

: [Examples of the cat are tiger lion and puma]
: matches [Examples of the ^family are ^^examples] =>
** <false>
```

(Notice that the second call of matches returns <false> as the list examples is
not [tiger lion and puma], it is [lion tiger and puma].)

5.1.2 Matching templates

The operator matches does not have to be provided with completely
specified lists. Instead, it allows the possibility of matching a list with a
template. The template always appears to the right of the matches operator, in the following form:

    LIST matches TEMPLATE

A template is some representation of a list, which need not be fully
specified, i.e. it may contain elements whose value we do not know. In
the syntax of matches, an equals sign, =, found in the right hand list,
matches any one element in the left hand list. Hence:

    : [helium oxygen neon sodium] matches [helium oxygen neon =] =>
    ** <true>
    : [1 4 9 16] matches [1 = 9 =] =>
    ** <true>
    : [rat mouse beaver] matches [rat mouse = beaver] =>
    ** <false>

The equals sign (pronounced 'gobble' in matching jargon) matches *exactly
one* element of a list. This is why the last example returns <false>, there
is no word between "mouse" and "beaver" in the left hand list. Furthermore:

    : [the tempest] matches [the tempest =] =>
    ** <false>

This result occurs because there is no word after "tempest" in the left hand
list.

    You may use as many gobbles as you like in a list template, but
remember, each gobble matches exactly one list element. Of course, this
element may be any of the usual data structures. Hence:

    : [one two [three four] 5] matches [= two = =] =>
    ** <true>

The left hand list here contains four elements, the second of which is the
word "two". As this is exactly the form of the template, the operator
returns <true>.

    There is a more general version of the gobble facility. This is written
as two equals signs with no intervening space, ==, and is pronounced
'gobble any'. The gobble any sign matches *any* number of elements in a
list, including none at all. Hence:

```
: Chelium oxygen neon sodium argon] matches Chelium == argon] =>
** <true>
: [1 4 9 16] matches [== 1 4 9 ==] =>
** <true>
: Crat mouse beaver] matches [== mouse] =>
** <false>
```

Notice that the final example returns <false> here. The template represents a list which ends with the word "mouse" but has any number of elements preceding this word. This is not the format of the left hand list – i.e. that list ends in "beaver", and not "mouse". Hence the operator returns <false>.

We could now define procedures using the matches operator. For example, consider a much easier definition of the procedure ismember, as defined recursively in Chapter 4.

```
define ismember(element,list);
if list matches [== ^element ==]
then true
else false
endif
enddefine;
```

(Can you spot an even shorter definition of ismember?) So,

```
: ismember("mike",Cdennis eric mike]) =>
** <true>

: vars fruit;
: Cbanana apple pear plum] -> fruit;
: ismember("plum",fruit) =>
** <true>
: ismember("tomato",fruit) =>
** <false>
```

5.1.3 Variable assignment in matching

In addition to allowing matching with the catch-all gobble signs, the matches operator also allows variable assignment in the list template. This is performed using the ? and ?? symbols. Consider the following:

```
: vars city;
: CThe Louvre is in Paris] matches CThe Louvre is in ?city] =>
** <true>
```

The use of the question-mark, followed by a variable name, in the template list has two effects. First the question-mark/variable symbol is interpreted as a gobble sign. The matches operator returns <true> or <false> in the usual way. Secondly, the matched item is assigned to the variable in the right hand list. So,

```
: city =>
** Paris
```

Read through the following examples and try to follow exactly what is happening in each one:

```
: vars x y;
: [one two [three four] 5] matches [one ?x ?y =] =>
** <true>
: x =>
** two
: y =>
** [three four]

: [a b c d e] matches [= ?x ==] =>
** <true>
: x =>
** b

: [one two three] matches [== ?x] =>
** <true>
: x =>
** three

: [one two three] matches [== ?x =] =>
** <true>
: x =>
** two

: [one two three] matches [= = = ?x] =>
** <false>
: x =>
** two
```

Notice that in the last example matching has failed, and the variable x has retained its old value. This is not always the case, variable assignment occurs element by element and so sometimes an assignment is made even when matches returns <false>.

The double question-mark symbol, ??, works analogously to the gobble-any symbol. That is, a double question-mark followed by a variable name is first treated as a == symbol. If matches returns <true> the elements which == would have matched are placed in a list, and this list is assigned to the variable name. Hence:

```
: vars x;
: [America England France Germany] matches [America England ??x] =>
```

```
** <true>
: x =>
** [France Germany]
```

As with gobble-any, this construction will match any number of elements, including none at all. If the construction matches zero elements the empty list, [], is assigned to the variable. Here are a few examples:

```
: vars x y z;
: [my friends are Eric George and Albert] matches [my ?x are ??y] =>
** <true>
: x =>
** friends
: y =>
** [Eric George and Albert]

: [a b [c d] e] matches [= ??x] =>
** <true>
: x =>
** [b [c d] e]

: [apple pear plum orange banana] matches [??x apple ??y ?z] =>
** <true>
: x =>
** []
: y =>
** [pear plum orange]
: z =>
** banana
```

As with the single question-mark, this variable assignment may take place if the matches operator returns <false>. Beware of this eventuality.

5.1.4 Some procedures using matches

Now we can look at some procedures using what we know of the matches operator so far. Consider a procedure which is to remove a given item from a given list:

```
define getrid(element,list);
vars before after;
if list matches [??before ^element ??after]
then [^^before ^^after]
else list
endif
enddefine;
```

So,

```
: getrid("a",[once upon a time]) =>
** [once upon time]
: getrid("lived",[once upon a time]) =>
** [once upon a time]
```

In this procedure the template opens with the ?? symbol. This converts everything preceding the target element to a list and assigns this list to the variable before. Similarly a list is created containing everything following the target element and this is assigned to the variable after. In the ACTION part of the procedure, the ^^ symbol is used to evaluate these variables and empty them into the same list. This is because we now have values for the variables, and the ^^ symbol forces their evaluation. Notice that an alternative to

```
[^^before ^^after]
```

would be

```
before <> after
```

these statements are equivalent in this example.

Here are some more examples.

```
define swap(list,el1,el2);
vars frontbit midbit backbit;
if list matches [??frontbit ^el1 ??midbit ^el2 ??backbit]
then [^^frontbit ^el2 ^^midbit ^el1 ^^backbit]
elseif list matches [??frontbit ^el2 ??midbit ^el1 ??backbit]
then [^^frontbit ^el1 ^^midbit ^el2 ^^backbit]
else [the two elements are not in the list]
endif
enddefine;
```

This procedure swaps the positions of two elements in a list. Hence:

```
: vars letters;
: [a b c d e] -> letters;
: swap(letters,"b","e") =>
** [a e c d b]
: swap(letters,"a","j") =>
** [the two elements are not in the list]
```

Here is another procedure definition. This one replaces an occurrence of a given element in a list, with another given element.

```
define substitute(elem1,elem2,list);
vars frontbit backbit;
if list matches [??frontbit ^elem2 ??backbit]
then [^^frontbit ^elem1 ^^backbit]
else list
```

```
    endif
    enddefine;
```

So,

```
: substitute("z","a",letters) =>
** [z b c d e]
```

However, what would happen if there were more than one occurrence of the target element?

```
: substitute("she","he",[he thought he was in America]) =>
** [she thought he was in America]
```

So the procedure has changed only the first instance of "he" to "she". Of course this might be what we want. However, if we actually wanted to replace all the instances of elem2 with elem1, we could change the procedure by simply assigning the result of the first substitution to a variable, and repeating the operation recursively. Hence:

```
    define substitute(elem1,elem2,list);
    vars frontbit backbit;
    if list matches [??frontbit ^elem2 ??backbit]
    then [^^frontbit ^elem1 ^^backbit] -> list;
         substitute(elem1,elem2,list)
    else list
    endif
    enddefine;
```

We have now made the procedure recursive. It will continue to call itself as long as there are instances of elem2 in the list. So,

```
: substitute("dee","ron",[da doo ron ron ron da doo ron ron]) =>
** [da doo dee dee dee da doo dee dee]
```

5.1.5 The matcharrow and conditional matching

There are two further facilities associated with matching in POP-11. The first is just a version of the matches operator which assumes a true match. This is an operator called the **matcharrow**, and is written -->. The matcharrow performs variable assignment and template matching in exactly the same way as the matches operator, but does not leave a <true> or <false> value on the stack. If there is no match, a MISHAP occurs. Hence:

```
: vars a b;
: [sparrow hawk eagle budgie thrush] --> [sparrow ?a eagle ??b];
: a =>
** hawk
```

```
: b =>
** [budgie thrush]

: [horse donkey mule] --> [= ??a];
: a =>
: [donkey mule]
: [hey diddle diddle] --> [hey = diddle ?a];
** MISHAP ...
```

When you know that there will be a successful match, and want to keep a clear notion of what is currently on the stack, it is sometimes useful to use this operator.

The second device allows conditional matching. This device is used when one wants to match a list with a template containing a match *only* if the template has some particular property. The best way to understand this is to follow an example. In the example, PROC stands for the name of an existing procedure.

```
: vars a;
: [one two three] matches [one ?a:PROC three];
```

This match only returns <true> if PROC("two") returns <true>.. First the match for ?a is found and the variable assignment is made. Next, this value is sent as an argument to the already defined procedure following the colon. If this procedure, with this argument, returns <true>, then matches returns <true>, otherwise matches returns <false>. Analogously, the construction

```
??a:PROC
```

requires that the *list* assigned to a, is sent as an argument to PROC, which must then return <true>. We find that use of conditional matching can lead to confusion, and so we will not use this device in the rest of the book. However, if you read other people's programs you will come across it, and so it's worth knowing about.

5.2 The database

The **database** in POP-11, as its name suggests, is a place where information may be stored. There are pre-defined procedures which make operations on this stored information very simple, and we will introduce the important operations in this section.

The database is stored in a global variable called database. Each time you enter the POP-11 system, database is initialized as the empty list. So check that the variable exists:

```
: database =>
** []
```

Now, the elements, or data that we store in the database are usually themselves lists. In fact, all the database structures which we will discuss use data in lists. The first thing you need to know is how to get data into the database. This is done using the pre-defined procedure add, which takes one argument. Try this:

```
: add([Shakespeare wrote The Tempest]);
```

This procedure does not return any result, but adds its argument to the database. So:

```
: database =>
** [[Shakespeare wrote The Tempest]]
```

We could now add some other piece of information:

```
: add([Shaw wrote Major Barbara]);
```

Now we can see how this procedure execution has affected the database:

```
: database =>
** [[Shaw wrote Major Barbara] [Shakespeare wrote The Tempest]]
```

You can see, then, that add inserts its argument into the head of the database. Were it not a pre-defined procedure, we could have defined add thus:

```
define add(arg);
[ ^arg ^^database] -> database
enddefine;
```

If you keep adding lists to the database, you will soon discover that inspecting its content by use of the printarrow is unsatisfactory. For example,

```
: add([Brecht wrote Mother Courage]);
: add([Ibsen wrote Peer Gynt]);
: add([Wilde wrote The Importance of being Ernest]);
: database =>
** [ [Wilde wrote the Importance of being Ernest] [Ibsen wrote
 Peer Gynt] [Brecht wrote Mother Courage] [Shaw
 wrote Major Barbara] [Shakespeare wrote The Tempest] ]
```

For easy inspection of large lists, there is a version of the printarrow which prints in a more readable form. This is called the pretty printarrow and is written ==>. Hence:

```
: database ==>
** [ [Wilde wrote the Importance of being Ernest]
     [Ibsen wrote Peer Gynt]
     [Brecht wrote Mother Courage]
     [Shaw wrote Major Barbara]
     [Shakespeare wrote The Tempest] ]
```

So the database is just a list. You may perform any of the usual operations on this list and, furthermore, the procedure add adds an element to the front of the list. In this instance (and in all following examples) we have added *lists* to the database, and so the database becomes a list of lists.

In addition to add there is a procedure for removing elements from the database. This is called remove, and follows the same syntax as add. Hence:

```
: remove([Shaw wrote Major Barbara]);
: database ==>
** [ [Wilde wrote the Importance of being Ernest]
     [Ibsen wrote Peer Gynt]
     [Brecht wrote Mother Courage]
     [Shakespeare wrote The Tempest] ]
```

If you provide remove with an argument which is not an element of the database, you will cause a MISHAP. This can be a nuisance if you do not know the full specification of the target list. For this reason, it is a useful feature of database procedures that they can use *matching* syntax. Hence:

```
: remove([Wilde ==]);
: database ==>
** [ [Ibsen wrote Peer Gynt]
     [Brecht wrote Mother Courage]
     [Shakespeare wrote The Tempest] ]
```

Of course, if the pattern provided as an argument to remove is not present in the database a MISHAP is generated. For example,

```
: remove([Brecht wrote =]);
** MISHAP ...
```

So these built-in procedures add and remove form the simplest means of operating on the database. As well as procedures for changing the database, there exist further procedures for interrogating it – i.e. finding out whether elements are present in the database or not. The simplest procedures for doing this are present and lookup.

The procedure present takes one argument and returns <true> if this argument is in the database, and <false> if it is not. (On some systems present returns the matched item if a match is made. However, this does not affect the use of present in conditionals, as any value which is not <false> is taken to be equivalent to <true>.) As present is a pre-defined procedure you do not need to define it yourself. However, it could have been defined like this:

```
define present(arg);
database matches [== ^arg ==]
enddefine;
```

Here are a few examples of its use – assuming that the database is in the same state as we left it after the last set of operations:

```
: present([Ibsen wrote Peer Gynt]) =>
** <true>

: present([Ibsen]) =>
** <false>
```

present also allows matching notation, so:

```
: present([Ibsen ==]) =>
** <true>
```

It can also be used in variable assignment, as with the matches operator. So:

```
: vars author play;
: present([?author wrote The Tempest]) =>
** <true>
: author =>
** Shakespeare

: present([Brecht wrote ??play]) =>
** <true>
: play =>
** [Mother Courage]

: present([?author wrote ^^play]) =>
** <true>
: author =>
** Brecht

: present([Wilde wrote ??play]) =>
** <false>
: play =>
** [Mother Courage]
```

Notice that the last execution of present returns a <false> value. Hence the variable play retains its previous value.

The procedure lookup works in exactly the same way as present with the exception that it returns no value. We only use lookup if we know that the target item is present in the database, and if we wish to make use of the variable assignment properties of the matching facility. If its argument is not present in the database, lookup will cause a MISHAP. It could be defined:

```
define lookup(arg);
database --> [== ^arg ==]
enddefine;
```

So:

```
: vars a;
: lookup([Ibsen ?a Peer Gynt]);
: a =>
** wrote

: lookup([Ibsen wrote ?a Peer Gynt]);
MISHAP ...
```

It is often useful to use lookup when we do not want to clutter the stack with <true> and <false> values.

Using these built-in procedures we could now write some of our own procedures to operate on this database. To use with the example of a set of authors and their plays we could write the following procedures:

```
define whowrote(play);
vars auth;
if present([?auth wrote ^^play])
then auth
else [play not known]
endif
enddefine;

define whatwrote(person);
vars work;
if  present([^person wrote ??work])
then work
else [author not known]
endif
enddefine;
```

Hence:

```
: whowrote([Peer Gynt]) =>
** Ibsen

: whatwrote("Shakespeare") =>
** [The Tempest]
```

Now let's increase the database store:

```
: add([Shakespeare wrote Hamlet]);
: add([Shakespeare wrote The Taming of the Shrew]);
: add([Ibsen wrote Hedda Gabler]);
```

So,

```
: database ==>
** [ [Ibsen wrote Hedda Gabler]
    [Shakespeare wrote The Taming of the Shrew]
    [Shakespeare wrote Hamlet]
    [Ibsen wrote Peer Gynt]
    [Brecht wrote Mother Courage]
    [Shakespeare wrote The Tempest] ]
```

Now let's try whatwrote again:

```
: whatwrote("Shakespeare") =>
** [The Taming of the Shrew]
```

In this example only the first instance of "Shakespeare" is picked up. This is because present only finds the first instance of the pattern provided as its argument. There is a built-in mechanism for finding *all* items in a database which match a given pattern, and this is called the foreach loop. The structure of a foreach loop is as follows:

```
foreach PATTERN
do    ACTION
endforeach;
```

So here is a more elaborate version of the whatwrote procedure, incorporating a foreach loop:

```
define whatwrote(person);
vars work;
foreach [^person wrote ??work]
do work =>
endforeach
enddefine;
```

This procedure searches through the database looking for a match for the list [^person wrote ??work]. Every time such a match is made, the part of the list following "wrote" is assigned to the variable work and the system moves on to do the operations described in the ACTION part of the program. When these are done, the system moves on to the next match. So:

```
: whatwrote("Shakespeare");
** [The Taming of the Shrew]
** [Hamlet]
** [The Tempest]
```

In fact, there is a global variable called it which is set to the value of the database element most recently matched by the facilities described in this section. Try this:

```
: lookup([Brecht ==]);
: it =>
** [Brecht wrote Mother Courage]
```

The global variable it is set to the match made by remove, present, lookup and foreach and can sometimes come in handy.

Now our database is becoming a little unwieldy. Let's write a procedure to tidy up repeated information:

```
define collect(writer);
vars play allworks;
[] -> allworks;
foreach [^writer wrote ??play]
do   [^^allworks ^play] -> allworks;
     remove(it)
endforeach;
add([^writer wrote ^^allworks])
enddefine;
```

Can you see what this procedure does? Try it.

```
: collect("Ibsen");
: database ==>
** [ [Ibsen wrote [Hedda Gabler] [Peer Gynt] ]
    [Shakespeare wrote Hamlet]
    [Shakespeare wrote The Taming of the Shrew]
    [Brecht wrote Mother Courage]
    [Shakespeare wrote The Tempest] ]
```

We could go on writing clever extensions to this database for ever. However, the major points have now been made, and all the important database operations have been introduced. One point which should be made here is that the structure of your database will determine the structure of the procedures which you write to operate upon it. The representation of playwrights which we chose here is by no means the only one available, and you should not think that this form of representation necessarily suits your needs best. For instance, we could have written the database in this form:

```
: add([ [playwright William Shakespeare]
    [birth 1564 death 1616]
    [plays [The Tempest] [Hamlet] [The Taming of the Shrew]] ]);

: add([ [playwright George Bernard Shaw]
    [birth 1856 death 1950]
    [plays [Major Barbara] [Pygmalion]] ]);
```

and so on. Had we chosen such a representation, our definitions of whatwrote and whowrote would look rather different (try to re-define them to operate on this form of database).

If we do not care about the form of representation of information for our programs, then we would choose the simplest representation available. However, sometimes we want to constrain our information to be stored in a particular manner. An example of this would be when we wanted to construct a computer model of some process, and we know (or assert) that the information for this process should be stored in a particular manner. In these cases, we must be careful to structure the database in accordance with such constraints. We will discuss these ideas further in Chapter 8.

We have seen that the database is a powerful means of storing and representing information. However there is nothing special about the POP-11 implementation of the database – it is just that people have already written procedures to help you manipulate a variable called database. In fact, you could write all the facilities yourself to operate on some other list (called any other variable name). Instead of thinking of the database as a further mysterious entity in the language, you could just remember that it is like any list, but that someone has written your early procedures for you.

EXERCISES

5.1 Use the matches operator to write a procedure which takes a pair of lists and returns the elements which are not in both lists.

5.2 Use the matches operator to write a procedure which takes a list and returns every alternate element of that list. (Hint: make it recursive.)

5.3 Construct a database to represent your diary. Write procedures to check what you should be doing at a particular time, add new information and query impossible timetabling.

Chapter 6 More Advanced Facilities

6.1 Introduction

The purpose of this chapter is not to introduce new programming concepts. Rather, it is intended as a brief survey of some useful facilities available in POP-11 which have not so far been discussed. As we pointed out in Chapter 1, it would be pointless to try to provide a complete specification of POP-11 in a book like this. However, the reader may benefit from having certain features illustrated at this stage. We will not discuss any of these facilities in much detail. Documentation is available and the advanced programmer will want to follow this up. For those new to programming, this chapter simply points to some disparate features which may come in useful as you start to build more complex programs.

6.2 Writing interactive programs

In Chapter 4 we gave an example procedure called `capital`. To refresh your memory, here it is again:

```
define capital(country);
if country = "England"
then [the capital of England is London]
elseif country = "USA"
then [the capital of USA is Washington]
elseif country = "Australia"
then [the capital of Australia is Canberra]
else [I dont know the capital of ^country]
endif
enddefine;
```

To execute this procedure we had to provide a word as an argument to the procedure. For example,

```
: capital("Belgium") =>
** [I dont know the capital of Belgium]
```

There exists a facility in POP-11 which allows for **interactive** assignment of objects to variables. The built-in procedures for doing this are called itemread and readline. First we will consider itemread. This procedure takes no arguments, and instructs the system to read the next item of input directly from the terminal. This input can be used in a variety of ways. Here is a typical usage for itemread:

```
: vars inp;
: itemread() -> inp;
: 4
: inp =>
** 4
```

The second line of this example can be taken to mean: read the next item typed onto the terminal, and assign it to the variable inp. We can see on the third and fifth lines that this is exactly what happens.

As its name suggests, itemread will read only one item. It assumes that this will be either a word or a number. For this reason you do not have to enclose word inputs with double quotation marks – they would be redundant. So:

```
: itemread() -> inp;
: mike
: inp =>
** mike
```

Using this procedure we could make our capital program much more 'friendly' by providing an interactive 'front-end'. Here is a front-end procedure:

```
define speak();
vars input;
[what country do you want to know about] =>
itemread() -> input;
capital(input) =>
enddefine;
```

Here is an example of the procedure execution:

```
: speak();
** [what country do you want to know about]
: USA
** [the capital of USA is Washington]
```

A short, though more difficult to read, version of this procedure would look like this:

```
define speak();
[what country do you want to know about] =>
capital(itemread()) =>
enddefine;
```

This procedure is functionally equivalent to the first definition. The third line simply says, do capital on the result of doing itemread. The format you choose is entirely up to you – many students find the first definition easier and there is no reason why you should not use that format. However, if you read other people's programs you will sometimes come across the latter format.

The second input procedure, readline, has the same format as itemread, but reads in lists. The procedure reads everything on the next line and puts it into a list. You do not have to provide the list brackets in your input. You will notice that readline gives you a different prompt – the question-mark.

```
: readline() -> inp;
? the loveliness of Paris
: inp =>
** [the loveliness of Paris]
```

An example of a procedure using readline would be an interactive front-end to the whowrote procedure as defined in the last chapter:

```
define askauthor();
vars play;
[type the name of the play] =>
readline() -> play;
whowrote(play) =>
enddefine;
```

We could extend procedures like the two above to simulate a conversation between system and user which can go on as long as the user wishes. For example, consider an extension of askauthor:

```
define askauthor();
vars play;
[This is a procedure to tell you the author of a given play] =>
[When you want to stop type stop] =>
until play = [stop]
do  [type the name of the play] =>
    readline() -> play;
    whowrote(play) =>
enduntil;
[thank you and goodbye] =>
enddefine;
```

Assuming that we had set up the database in the same format as in the last chapter, an interaction with this procedure would look like this:

```
: askauthor();
** [This is a procedure to tell you the author of a given play]
```

```
** [When you want to stop type stop]
** [type the name of the play]
? The Taming of the Shrew
** Shakespeare
** [type the name of the play]
? Peer Gynt
** Ibsen
** [type the name of the play]
? stop
** [play not known]
** [thank you and goodbye]
```

Notice that this procedure forces an execution of whowrote with the argument [stop]; can you think of a way to avoid this? (Hint: you might need two procedures.)

It is often the case that we want to build procedures which not only work, but which provide a sensible interface with the user. When you want to build the interface in a sensible manner, itemread and readline are very useful procedures.

6.3 and and or

In addition to procedure definitions, POP-11 can encode a set of instructions as an **operation**. The difference between a procedure and an operation is a superficial one. Operations designed to work on two arguments are called with 'infix' notation, that is, they appear between their two arguments. We have already met the operations +, -, -->, etc. If these were defined as procedures, they would have to be called with 'prefix notation', that is +(3,4). There are two further built-in operators which we have not mentioned so far, but which come in very useful when building large programs. These are called and and or. These are both infix operators which return <true> or <false> values.

The and operator returns <true> if the value of *both* its arguments is <true>, otherwise it returns <false>. The or operator returns <true> if the value of *at least one* of its arguments is <true>, otherwise it returns <false>. The following trivial examples illustrate this:

```
: 3+4 = 7 and 3-2 = 1 =>
** <true>

: length([1 2 3]) = 3 and hd([a b c]) = "b" =>
** <false>

: length([1 2 3]) = 3 or hd([a b c]) = "b" =>
** <true>
```

```
: 3 = 2 or 9+1 = 8 =>
** <false>
```

These examples are all rather obvious and it might seem that there can be little use for these operators. However, they can be very useful in certain procedure definitions, particularly those involving conditionals. As an example, consider a procedure which takes three lists as arguments and returns the first element common to all three lists:

```
define isinall(L1,L2,L3);
if L1 = []
then [no common word]
elseif L2 matches [== ^(hd(L1)) ==]
       and L3 matches [== ^(hd(L1)) ==]
then hd(L1)
else isinall(tl(L1),L2,L3)
endif
enddefine;
```

Notice that the two arguments to and have to be complete statements which return a <true> or <false> value. A common error is to use and in the following way:

```
elseif L2 and L3 matches [== ^(hd(L1)) ==]
```

This is true if L2 is <true> and if

```
L3 matches [== ^(hd(L1)) ==]
```

returns <true>. So you can see that it would be an inappropriate use here.

6.4 Updaters

Consider the following POP-11 code:

```
: vars x;
: [one two three four] -> x;
: hd(x) =>
** one
```

So far nothing surprising has happened. A variable has been declared and a list assigned to it. The parts of the list can be accessed using various procedures, of which hd is an example. However, procedures can also be used to *change* the various parts of the list. Consider the following:

```
: "seven" -> hd(x);
: x =>
** [seven two three four]
```

This is a new use of procedures – so far we have found them only on the left of the assignment arrow. In this example, however, we have used the procedure hd on the right of the assignment arrow in order to insert an item into a list. This is possible because the procedure hd has an **updater** associated with it. An updater allows you to use a procedure to insert items into a structure. The POP-11 system automatically uses the updater of a procedure if it finds that procedure on the right of an assignment arrow.

As you might expect, tl also has an updater. So,

```
: [eight nine] -> tl(x);
: x =>
** [seven eight nine]
```

Furthermore the procedure x (i.e. the name of a list used for numbered access) has an updater. So,

```
: [horse sheep] -> x(2);
: x =>
** [seven [horse sheep] nine]
```

When you define your own procedures there will not be an updater automatically written for you. For example, imagine you had written a procedure to return the third item of a list:

```
define third(list);
hd(tl(tl(list)))
enddefine;
```

Now, if you tried to use the updater of this procedure you would get a MISHAP:

```
: vars x;
: [a b c d] -> x;
: "f" -> third(x);
MISHAP ...
```

If you want to provide an updater for your procedure you may do so using updaterof. Here is an example for third:

```
define updaterof third(value,list);
value -> hd(tl(tl(list)))
enddefine;
```

Note the position of updaterof, this tells the system that you are defining an updater for third rather than third itself. You may now use the updater as usual:

```
: "f" -> third(x);
: x =>
** [a b f d]
```

6.5 Further datatypes

The examples used in this book so far have included only three explicit types of data object (called datatypes); these are numbers, words and lists. There are, in fact, other types of objects in POP-11, though these are not used as often as those introduced to date. We shall give a brief account of two new datatypes here: **strings** and **arrays**. We shall then reveal the use of procedures as datatypes.

6.5.1 Strings

A string comprises any set of characters, delimited by single quotations marks ('). It is similar to a word, in that it is usually considered to be a unitary object (unlike a list which is a set of objects). However, it is different from a word in that it may contain spaces, and other non-alphanumeric characters. So:

```
'hello goodbye'
```

is a string of 13 characters. (Be sure to use the same quotation mark – the close quote – at both ends of the string. The open quote has a quite different meaning.)

The main use of strings occurs in formatting output. There is a built-in procedure called pr which takes one argument and prints that argument on the screen. Unlike the printarrow, the output is not followed by a new line and there are no output stars. Try the following:

```
: pr(3);
3:
```

The colon prompt now appears on the same line as the output. In order to force a new line to be printed, we need to use the procedure nl. This procedure takes one argument, a number, and prints that many new lines on the screen. Hence:

```
: pr(3);nl(1);
3
:
```

Now, pr can take any datatype as its argument (or, of course, a variable name). When used with a list, pr prints out just that list, for example,

```
: pr([one two three]);
[one two three]:
```

There is another procedure, ppr, which will not print the list brackets of a list given as argument, for example,

```
: ppr([one two three]);
one two three:
```

The procedure pr is particularly useful when used with strings as this allows some control over the output format. Consider the following examples:

```
: ppr([Left                 Right]);nl(1);
Left Right
:
: pr('Left                  Right');nl(1);
Left                Right
:
```

In the first line we want to print the list given. However, spaces in lists are not preserved – they do not have any meaning. Hence the output does not contain the spaces originally typed. Spaces in strings are legitimate characters and so they are reflected in the output. (If you have an old version of POP-11 you will find that the string quotes are printed by pr. This can be avoided using the ppr procedure on strings.)

As an example of a formatting procedure consider the following:

```
define pops(china,usa,france,uk,sweden);
nl(2);pr('     Populations of various countries (millions)');nl(2);
pr('China              ');pr(china);nl(1);
pr('America            ');pr(usa);nl(1);
pr('France             ');pr(france);nl(1);
pr('United Kingdom     ');pr(uk);nl(1);
pr('Sweden             ');pr(sweden);nl(1);
enddefine;
```

We could execute this procedure as follows:

```
: pops(1000,200,60,55,7);

     Populations of various countries (millions)

China              1000
America            200
France             60
United Kingdom     55
Sweden             7
```

Can you think of a way of extending this program so that the numbers are presented with the thousands, hundreds, tens and units columns aligned? Make your extension as general as possible so that the columns are aligned whatever the input.

6.5.2 Arrays

An array is a data object which may have more than one dimension. Here is a representation of a two-dimensional array:

a b c
d e f

This array has three columns and two rows; it is conventionally referred to as a 3×2 array. A one-dimensional array might be represented like this:

a b c d

It is harder to represent a three-dimensional array on paper but you could imagine the idea of adding layers to that of rows and columns given in the 3×2 array. In that case a three-dimensional array could be represented like this:

layer 1   layer 2

a b c   g h i
d e f   j k l

Although we tend predominantly to use lists in POP-11, there are instances when arrays provide a simpler representation.

To make an array, a procedure called newarray is provided. This procedure takes two arguments, first a list containing the dimensions of the array, and second the value of all the initial array elements. The second argument is easy to understand. When you make an array in POP-11 you have to specify what all the initial elements are to be, and these are set to the value of the second argument – whether it be a word, a number, a list or whatever else.

The first argument to newarray is more difficult to understand if you have not encountered arrays before. First you have to decide how many dimensions you want your array to have. For the sake of an example we'll make the 3×2 array described above. Now, each dimension has a given number of *levels*, i.e. instances on that dimension. In the 3×2 array the first dimension has 3 levels and the second dimension has 2 levels. In POP-11, each level of a dimension is referred to by a number. The dimensions list given as an argument to newarray gives information about what these index numbers are to be called. The list contains two numbers for each dimension, one specifying the reference number of the first level, and one specifying the reference number of the last level on that dimension. An example will help at this stage:

```
: vars myarr;
: newarray([1 3 1 2],"a") -> myarr;
```

This means: make a two-dimensional array called myarr; the first dimension has three levels, indexed by the numbers 1, 2, 3; the second dimension has two levels, indexed by the numbers 1 and 2; all elements start their life with the value "a".

We can now access the various elements of myarr by providing arguments to the array name in the same way as we can access lists numerically. So:

```
: myarr(2,2) =>
** a
```

This means: print the value of the array element found at the second level of the first dimension and the second level of the second dimension. Try to access another element of the array:

```
: myarr(3,1) =>
** a
```

Of course, all the elements of the array are initially set to "a" in this example and so the above should not be surprising. We can alter the value of array elements by making use of the fact that the procedure with the name of the array is automatically provided with an updater (see Section 6.4). So,

```
: "b" -> myarr(2,1);
: "c" -> myarr(3,1);
```

The first line means: set the value of the second level of the first dimension and the first level of the second dimension to "b". So,

```
: myarr(1,1) =>
** a
: myarr(2,1) =>
** b
: myarr(3,1) =>
** c
```

The dimensions list of an array does not have to include dimensions starting at index 1. So,

```
: vars myarr2;
: newarray([-3 3 10 100],0) -> myarr2;
```

This command means: make a two-dimensional array called myarr2; the first dimension has 7 levels, indexed by the numbers -3 to +3; the second dimension has 91 levels, indexed by the numbers 10 to 100; all elements start life with the value 0. So:

```
: myarr2(-2,81) =>
** 0
```

To increase the number of dimensions of an array, we can simply increase the length of the dimensions list. The following example would create a particular four-dimensional array:

```
: vars arragain;
: newarray([1 10 1 10 0 5 0 8],"z") -> arragain;
```

You may find that you very rarely need arrays; indeed lists can equally well be used to represent *n*-dimensional spaces by embedding them in

each other. However, arrays are sometimes the easiest way to characterize a particular set of data, and you should be aware of their existence.

6.5.3 Procedures as data objects

In addition to the standard types of objects mentioned so far, POP-11
treats procedures themselves as data objects. This means that you can use
procedures in a flexible way: for example by embedding them as elements
in lists. As an example, the following is a perfectly acceptable list:

```
: vars y;
: [one 7 ^hd 3 ^tl hd] -> y;
```

Notice that the procedures have to be prefixed by the 'hat' symbol in order
to distinguish them from words. So,

```
: y(3)([one two three]) =>
** one

: y(6)([one two three]) =>
MISHAP ...
```

This facility may come in handy if, for example, you wanted to apply
a set of procedures to one set of data. For example:

```
define doall(procs,list);
until procs = []
do    hd(procs)(list);
      tl(procs) -> procs
enduntil
enddefine;
```

So,

```
: doall([^hd ^tl ^rev],[1 2 3]) =>
** 1 [2 3] [3 2 1]
```

Although this facility will probably not be used by the novice, it can make
for very flexible programs – an important requirement when building large
systems.

6.6 Record classes

In addition to the types of objects we have already met (words, lists, etc.)
POP-11 allows you to invent your own types of objects. These are known
as **record classes**. The facility recordclass not only allows you to make
new classes of objects, but also provides you with some very helpful procedures for operating on these classes. As an example, imagine that you
wanted to define a class 'animals' which would allow you to access and use
information only about animals. Here is a possible format:

```
: recordclass animal legs diet origin;
```

This command says create a new class called animal. Each member of the class has a number of legs, a diet and an origin which should be specified. There can be any number of these specifications for a given record class. Now we have created the class, we need to make some records of this class. We can do this by use of the procedure consanimal (cons followed by the name of the class) which has been created for you by the call of recordclass. So,

```
: vars bear chimp;
: consanimal(4,"herbivore","Europe") -> bear;
: consanimal(2,"omnivore","Africa") -> chimp;
```

In addition to consanimal a number of extra procedures have now been created for you: destanimal leaves all the characteristics of its argument on the stack. So,

```
: destanimal(chimp) =>
** 2 omnivore Africa
```

The procedure isanimal returns <true> or <false> according to whether its argument is a member of the class animal or not:

```
: isanimal(chimp) =>
** <true>
: isanimal(giraffe) =>
** <false>
```

We also have procedures legs, diet and origin which return the corresponding value of their argument. So,

```
: legs(chimp) =>
** 2
: diet(bear) =>
** herbivore
```

These three procedures are automatically provided with updaters. So,

```
: 3 -> legs(chimp);
: destanimal(chimp) =>
** 3 omnivore Africa
```

Once again, we should say that the facility to define your own record classes will probably only be used by the advanced programmer. When building very large scale AI programs it is sometimes useful to define the possible elements of the programs so that they are specific to that particular application. However, such programs are beyond the scope of this book and you will not encounter this facility again. Readers who would like a more formal treatment of record classes should consult their system documentation.

6.7 Properties and associations

Imagine you wanted to store information about the nationality of various historical figures as part of a larger POP-11 program. You could do this by constructing a database (say) of two-element lists each containing the name and nationality of a person. These lists could then be accessed via the normal database procedures. However, POP-11 provides a simple and efficient way of storing item/value associations in what is called a **property table**. To create a property table we use the procedure newassoc in the following way:

```
: vars nationality;
: newassoc([[Napoleon French] [Newton British] [Marx German]])
    -> nationality;
```

We can now access the properties in the following way:

```
: nationality("Newton") =>
** British
```

Furthermore, we can add new associations by means of an updater. So,

```
: "Roman" -> nationality("Caesar");
: nationality("Caesar") =>
** Roman
```

Notice that the association is one-directional. So,

```
: nationality("French") =>
** <false>
```

This example also shows that the default value for a non-existent association is <false>.

The way in which these associations are stored is very efficient in computer-time. This means that people writing programs using large amounts of this type of data prefer to use newassoc rather than a more indirect way of associating items with properties. For those who are concerned about computer-time there is a procedure newproperty which allows you to specify exactly how the associations are stored in the computer. However, ordinary mortals need not worry about this and we recommend that more sophisticated programmers follow this up in the system documentation. For most purposes newassoc is perfectly adequate.

You have now reached the end of the introductory course in POP-11. Although there is much more to the language than we have discussed in these five chapters, you are perfectly well equipped to write respectable AI programs in POP-11. In the next section you will be presented with certain issues in AI, and shown how to write programs to deal with them. Hopefully, you will find that the ideas presented so far begin to come together in the context of larger working programs.

Part Two

Artificial Intelligence in POP-11

Chapter 7 **Problem Solving**

Problem solving is one of the most researched areas in AI. Indeed, it has a special historical place in the development of the discipline – one of the earliest and most influential AI models was a 'general problem solver' (see Newell and Simon, 1963; and Chapter 9, this volume). In this chapter we will introduce the basic ideas in problem solving and develop POP-11 programs to solve the same problem in two different ways. Before we do this, however, you need to have some understanding of what is meant by a problem in this context.

7.1 Problems

Here are some examples of the kind of problem which workers in AI have traditionally studied.

The Tower of Hanoi

You have an arrangement of three discs and three poles such that each disc has a hole in the middle and may be placed on any pole. The three discs are all different sizes. In the starting position all the discs occupy the left-most pole, the largest disc being on the bottom of the pile and the smallest on the top. Your task is to move one disc at a time until all the discs occupy the right-most pole in the same arrangement (see Figure 7.1). You are subject to the constraint that at no time must a disc be on top of a smaller disc.

The eights problem

In this problem, which you may have seen as a child's toy, a set of eight tiles is arranged on a 3×3 surface (see Figure 7.2). You may slide any tile into an adjacent space. The problem is to do this until you reach some specified end state such as the one illustrated.

The water jug problem

You have two water jugs and an endless supply of water from a tap. The jugs hold 4 and 3 pints of water respectively; neither jug has any

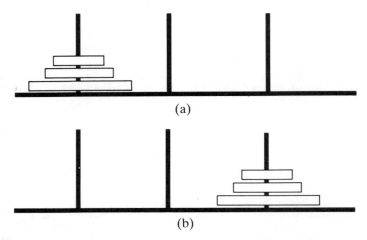

Figure 7.1 The Tower of Hanoi problem (a) the start state and (b) the goal state.

measuring marks. You may perform any of the following operations with the jugs: fill one or the other with water from the tap; fill one from the other; empty either on the ground. You start with both jugs empty and the problem is to get exactly 2 pints of water into the 4-pint jug.

Each of these problems is rather artificial in its own way. However, attempts to examine various strategies for solving them have produced a great deal of insight into solutions of practical problems. For example, imagine that you are an electrician searching for a fault in a very large electric circuit. Where do you start to look for the fault? If you can devise a technique which will make your search as quick as possible, you will save a great deal of time and effort.

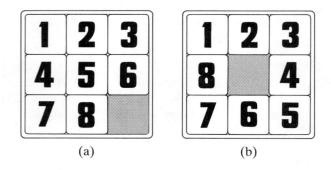

Figure 7.2 The eights problem (a) the start state and (b) the goal state.

As an exercise, try to solve each of the above problems with a pencil and paper. As you go through the steps to your solution, try to observe your own behaviour – do you try to solve these problems in broadly the same way?

In this chapter we will look at two ways (or **strategies**) of solving the water jug problem. (This problem, and a more detailed coverage of problem solving in general, can be found in Rich, 1983.) At the end of the chapter you might like to think about whether either of the strategies is similar to the strategies employed by humans. You might also think about how we could test the assertion that we have modelled human behaviour in our programs.

7.2 Problem spaces

The idea of a **problem space** (also called a search space or state space) is a powerful one in problem solving. A problem space is defined as a set of *states* that your world can be in at any one time. In a well structured representation of a problem space, one can retrieve the path from first state to goal state. As we will later be writing POP-11 programs to solve the two jugs problem, we will use this problem as an example in the following discussion of problem spaces.

Before we explore the state space for the two jugs problem, we need to formalize the description of the problem. Let us call the 4-pint jug X, and the 3-pint jug Y. For a proper formalization of the problem we need to identify three things: (i) the starting state of the world under consideration; (ii) the goal state of the world; (iii) the possible transformations allowed in the world. In this example (i) and (ii) are easy to define. In specifying (iii), the possible transformations are conventionally enumerated as rules. From the initial, rather loose, definition of the problem, we can see that there will be six transformation rules available in this problem.

Here is a formal definition of the problem.

Initial state: X has 0; Y has 0.

Goal state: X has 2; Y has any amount.

Transformations: Rule 1. Fill X from tap.
Rule 2. Fill Y from tap.
Rule 3. Fill X from Y.
Rule 4. Fill Y from X.
Rule 5. Empty X on ground.
Rule 6. Empty Y on ground.

Notice that this is only a complete description if we assume the given information that X has a capacity of 4 pints and Y has a capacity of 3 pints.

We can now start to explore the state space of this problem. Imagine applying all the rules to the initial state and representing the resulting states as descendants of the original. This is shown graphically in Figure 7.3.

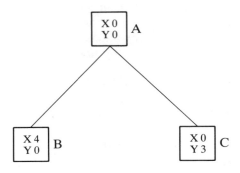

Figure 7.3 When we apply the rules to the initial state the resulting states can be shown as descendants of the original.

In this diagram we have chosen not to include the resultant states from rules which do not change the original state. So only rules 1 and 2 produce a change from the start state in this example. We have labelled the states A, B and C for ease of reference.

We could now expand this representation to include another level of the state space, that is the results of applying the rules to the bottom row of states. The result of doing this is shown in Figure 7.4.

So from state B, only rules 2, 4 and 5 produce changed states. From state C, only rules 1, 3 and 6 produce new states. Notice that states F and I are the same as state A. If we were to continue the process, the expanded space under F and I would look exactly like the space expanded under A. Therefore there is no point in continuing to expand states F and I, and so we drop them. The explored space can now be represented as shown in Figure 7.5.

A diagram like this is conventionally called a **tree**. Furthermore, individual paths through the tree, from top to bottom, are known as **branches**. So ABD is a branch, as is ACG.

We could continue to expand this diagram in exactly the same manner, row by row, until we find a state on the bottom row which corresponds to our required goal. By tracing the route from the start to the goal we would have found the shortest possible solution to our problem. (You might like to continue the exercise on paper in order to prove

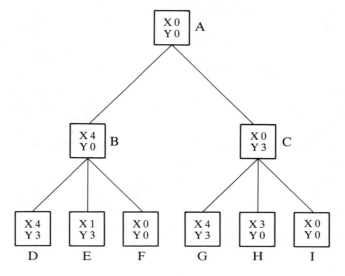

Figure 7.4 Expanding the representation of Figure 7.3.

to yourself that you do eventually reach the goal.) This method of searching a problem space is called a **breadth-first** search strategy. We will now compare this to another strategy – the **depth-first** strategy.

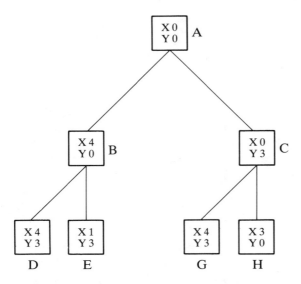

Figure 7.5 Representation of the explored space known as a 'tree'.

A depth-first strategy can be characterized like this:

1. From the start state, try all your transformation rules, in order, until you find one which produces a different state, then apply that rule. The resultant state now becomes your current state.

2. Next, try all your rules, in order again, until you find one that would lead to a state which has not already been visited, then apply that rule. The resultant state now becomes your current state.

3. Repeat (2) until you reach the goal state or until none of your rules leads to a novel state.

4. If no rules lead to a novel state, you have reached a dead-end. Revert to the state you were in before the present one and repeat (2).

You should note that this description of a depth-first search only works when you know that you will eventually reach the goal. If you are working on a problem which you think may not be solvable, you need to include some way of checking that you have not searched all the possible states without finding a solution.

The depth-first strategy is equivalent to exploring the problem space represented above, but following each branch to its bottom before looking at the next branch. So the first three steps of the depth-first search, using our example, are shown in Figure 7.6.

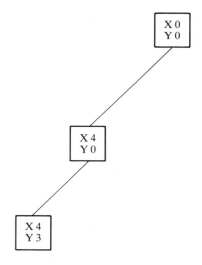

Figure 7.6 The depth-first strategy applied to exploration of the problem space.

Were we to reach dead-ends on some branches, the explored space might look as shown in Figure 7.7, where letters correspond to states.

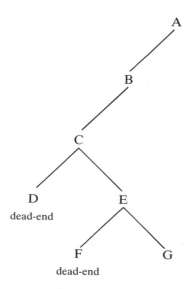

Figure 7.7 Some of the branches have resulted in dead-ends.

Thus you see that the depth-first strategy is just another way of exploring the same space as the breadth-first strategy, but in a different order. So what are the advantages and disadvantages of the two strategies?

In a breadth-first search you are guaranteed to find the quickest possible solution to your problem (i.e. the solution which requires the least number of steps); whereas, in a depth-first search, you may find a solution which is not necessarily the quickest. On the other hand, the breadth-first search means that you will definitely have to keep a record of a lot of information which will ultimately prove redundant – each step requires the creation of more and more states, and many of them will not be used in the eventual solution.

In fact, the choice between the two strategies depends on a number of things – particularly the sort of problem you are interested in. Factors which will affect your choice are: how many transformation rules have you got; how far away from the start is the goal likely to be; do you necessarily need the quickest solution, or just any solution to your problem?

In the next section we will build POP-11 programs to solve the jugs problem by depth- and breadth-first search strategies. Following that, we will discuss the strategies further, and give a brief overview of other search strategies which might be employed for this, and similar problems.

7.3 The programs

7.3.1 Representation of states

The first issue we need to confront when building a program to operate on some world (or domain), is how we are going to represent that world in POP-11. In this instance there is only a very small amount of information which we *need* to represent for each state – i.e. how many pints of water are currently in each jug. We need to choose a way of representing this state in POP-11, such that the transformation rules can easily 'discover' the state and act upon it appropriately. So we need a representation which we can easily access and transform.

Two forms of representation spring to mind: we could use the database, or we could use another global variable. If we choose to use the database, we might choose always to have two lists in it – one representing the contents of jug X, and one of jug Y. So the database might look like this:

```
: database =>
** [[jug X has 0 pints]
   [jug Y has 3 pints]]
```

We could then establish the contents of jug X, say, using the lookup command:

```
: vars x_contents;
: lookup([jug X has ?x_contents pints]);
: x_contents =>
** 0
```

Every time we changed the state of the world, we could remove the appropriate list from the database, and add a new one.

However, this seems like a very long-winded way of representing a very small amount of information. Instead, we could represent the state of the world as a simple two-element list. The first element of the list will represent the number of pints in jug X, and the second element the number of pints in jug Y.

In fact we *will* use this representation in what follows. It hardly seems worth employing the database to store such a limited amount of information, and so we will store the list as a global variable. Let us call it current. To initialize the world to the starting state, we could proceed as follows:

```
: vars current;
: [0 0] -> current;
```

We can easily access this list to discover the contents of either jug. For example, if we wanted to know the current contents of jug Y, we could perform the following operation:

```
: vars y_contents;
: current --> [= ?y_contents];
: y_contents =>
** 0
```

Notice that we have used the matcharrow here, rather than the matches operator. This is because we know that current does match a two-element list (the value of the template) and so we do not want to have a <true> or <false> value left around on the stack. We just want to make an assignment of a member of the list to a variable.

This issue of representation is one which needs to be decided upon right at the beginning of writing a program. This is simply because the way the subsequent program is written will depend on the particular representation which you choose. In what follows, we will use the global variable representation. You might like to think about how different the transformation rules would look if we had chosen to use the database facility for our representation.

7.3.2 The transformation rules

To remind you of the six rules we are dealing with in the jugs problem, here they are again:

Transformations: Rule 1. Fill X from tap.
Rule 2. Fill Y from tap.
Rule 3. Fill X from Y.
Rule 4. Fill Y from X.
Rule 5. Empty X on ground.
Rule 6. Empty Y on ground.

Now, how are we going to represent these rules in POP-11? Each rule will have to have access to the variable current. Let us decide now to make each rule return a list which represents the results of applying that rule to the current state.

Rules 1 and 2 seem to perform the same operation on the two jugs. To save time and effort, we could write one procedure to apply both rules. We could provide this procedure with an argument specifying which jug is to be filled from the tap. Let's call this procedure filltap. Here is a definition:

```
define filltap(jug);
vars x_cont y_cont;
current --> [?x_cont ?y_cont];
if jug = "x"
then [4 ^y_cont]
else [^x_cont 3]
endif
enddefine;
```

This procedure should be given arguments "x" or "y". On the third line it matches the variable current so that the local variables x_cont and y_cont can be set to the current contents of jugs X and Y respectively. If the argument passed to filltap is "x", the procedure returns a list representing a full jug X, and leaving the contents of jug Y alone. Otherwise (i.e. if the argument to filltap is "y"), the procedure returns a list representing a full jug Y, with the contents of jug X left alone. Let's try it out:

```
: [0 0] -> current;
: filltap("x") =>
** [4 0]
: filltap("y") =>
** [0 3]
```

If we wanted to change the value of current, we could assign it the result of performing filltap. For example,

```
: filltap("x") -> current;
: current =>
** [4 0]
: filltap("y") =>
** [4 3]
```

Notice that the filltap procedure works even if the jug is already full. In this case, the procedure simply returns a list which is the same as current. So:

```
: [4 1] -> current;
: filltap("x") =>
** [4 1]
```

We now have representations for rules 1 and 2 embodied in the same procedure. We now proceed to rules 3 and 4. Once again, these rules seem to be doing a similar job, that is, fill one jug from another. Let us think about exactly what these rules must do. Consider rule 3 first.

Rule 3 says fill jug X from jug Y. Now, if the contents of jug X plus those of jug Y will all fit into jug X (i.e. if the two jugs contain 4 or less pints between them), then we want to return a list with jug X containing the sum of the contents, and jug Y empty. On the other hand, if the contents of jug X plus those of jug Y are more than 4 pints, then we want to return a list with jug X represented as full, and jug Y containing the amount which will not fit into jug X. This could be done in the following way:

```
current --> [?xval ?yval];
if xval+yval > 4
then [4 ^(xval+yval-4)]
else [^(xval+yval) 0]
endif;
```

An exactly similar argument to this can be used when we want to apply rule 4 – though in this case we are concerned not to exceed the limit of jug Y, 3 pints.

We could combine rules 3 and 4 in one procedure. Let's call this procedure afromb and provide it with two arguments, juga and jugb. The first argument will represent the jug to be filled from the second argument. So we will allow the procedure to be called either as: afromb("x","y") or afromb("y","x"). Here is a definition:

```
define afromb(juga,jugb);
vars xval yval;
current --> [?xval ?yval];
if juga = "x"
then if xval+yval > 4
     then [4 ^(xval+yval-4)]
     else [^(xval+yval) 0]
     endif
else if yval+xval > 3
     then [^(xval+yval-3) 3]
     else [0 ^(xval+yval)]
     endif
endif
enddefine;
```

Notice that the second and third lines employ variables called xval and yval rather than x_cont and y_cont as in filltap. This is just to avoid any confusion which might arise by having two sets of variables called the same thing. In fact, as both sets are local variables they could be called the same names, but it is good practice to avoid this because debugging a program can become difficult if there is confusion about which variables belong where.

Let's try this procedure:

```
: [0 0] -> current;
: afromb("x","y") =>
** [0 0]

: [4 0] -> current;
: afromb("y","x") =>
** [1 3]

: [2 1] -> current;
: afromb("x","y") =>
** [3 0]
```

We now have only rules 5 and 6 left to deal with. These are very similar to rules 1 and 2. All we need to do is replace a jug's contents with zero. Here is a definition of a procedure empty which takes an argument "x" or "y" and returns a list in which the jug provided as argument is empty:

```
define empty(jugc);
vars xamount yamount;
current --> [?xamount ?yamount];
if jugc = "x"
then [0 ^yamount]
else [^xamount 0]
endif
enddefine;
```

Once again we have used different names for the local variables (jugc, xamount and yamount) to avoid any confusion in later stages. Let's make sure that this procedure does what it is supposed to do:

```
: [4 0] -> current;
: empty("x") =>
** [0 0]
: empty("y") =>
** [4 0]

: [2 3] -> current;
: empty("y") =>
** [2 0]
```

We now have all six rules encoded as POP-11. In the programs to search the problem space, it will make life easier for us if we can enumerate these as rules 1 to 6. Here is a simple program to label the rules:

```
define tryrule(num);
if num = 1
then filltap("x")
elseif num = 2
then filltap("y")
elseif num = 3
then afromb("x","y")
elseif num = 4
then afromb("y","x")
elseif num = 5
then empty("x")
elseif num = 6
then empty("y")
else [error] =>
endif
enddefine;
```

So we can now call the various rules by providing the appropriate number as an argument to tryrule; for example,

```
tryrule(1)
```

will call filltap("x") and so on. Furthermore, if we wanted to change the order of the rules, we could simply shuffle round the numbers in this procedure.

We are now in a position to write the search programs.

7.3.3 Depth-first search

Here is the algorithm for a depth-first search again:

1. From the start state, try all your transformation rules, in order, until you find one which produces a different state, then apply that rule. The resultant state now becomes your current state.

2. Next, try all your rules, in order again, until you find one that leads to a state which has not already been visited, then apply that rule. The resultant state now becomes your current state.

3. Repeat (2) until you reach the goal state or until none of your rules leads to a novel state.

4. If no rules lead to a novel state, you have reached a dead-end. Revert to the state you were in before the present one and repeat (2).

From this algorithm, you can see that we are going to need some way of checking which states have previously been visited. To do this, we will keep a record of all the states visited so far in a global variable, a list called history. To save us having to change current by hand all the time, let's define a procedure called dstartup which will initialize current and history to the starting state:

```
define dstartup();
[0 0] -> current;
[^current] -> history
enddefine;
```

So,

```
: dstartup();
: history =>
** [[0 0]]
```

At this stage history is a one-element list – it contains one state. As we add more states, history will be updated.

Now, to develop the depth-first search program, we are going to need careful planning. It is a good idea to build the program in stages first, before writing any code. Here is a first step towards specifying the program – we can combine programming notation with normal words in order to give us an idea as to how to proceed.

Initialize a variable A to 1

UNTIL goal is reached

DO try the A-th rule

      IF   the result is a state already visited

      THEN   increment A by 1

      ELSE   make the result the current state

              add that state to your history

              set A to 1 again

   ENDIF

ENDUNTIL

In this outline specification we keep track of which rule we are currently trying out by declaring a local variable, initializing it to 1, and then updating it as we need to. To fill it out a bit more, we could keep a note of the result of applying a rule in a temporary variable, without having to change current unnecessarily. Here is an initial attempt at a definition of this procedure, we'll call it depth:

```
1   define depth();
2   vars a next;
3   1 -> a;
4   until current matches [2 =]
5   do   tryrule(a) -> next;
6        if history matches [== ^next ==]
7        then a+1 -> a
8        else next -> current;
9             [^^history ^current] -> history;
10            1 -> a
11       endif
12  enduntil
13  enddefine;
```

We have given this program line numbers in order to be able to refer to it easily.

Line 4 represents the stopping condition. Remember, our aim is to end up with 2 pints in jug X and anything in jug Y. On line 5, rule a is tried (rule 1 in the first run-through) and the result sent to the variable next. Line 6 checks to see whether next has already been visited; if so, line 7 increments a by one, and the program leaves the IF clause. As there is nothing required of the program between the endif and the enduntil, the system now returns to line 4 with a new value of a. However, if line 6 returns <false> (i.e. we have generated a novel state), the system goes to line 8, where the variable current is updated to next. On line 9 this value is added to the history list, and on line 10 a is re-initialized to 1, so that when the program restarts the UNTIL loop, it will begin its attempt to find a way of expanding the current state by applying rule 1.

Will the program work? There is, in fact, a problem with it. The difficulty arises when none of the rules produces a novel state. In that case, a just gets bigger and bigger until it is so large that it does not provide a legal argument to the tryrule procedure.

In order to provide a facility for retracing one's steps from a dead-end, we need to add more to the program. In the revised program, the system will only operate on lines 5 to 11 if not all the rules have been tried on the present run-through. Otherwise, we want to go back to the previous state, add that state to the end of history again (so that in the final history you will be able to spot a dead-end because the state from which it was derived will be immediately returned to), and start the process again. Here is the revised program:

```
1  define depth();
2  vars a next previous;
3  1 -> a;
4  until current matches [2 =]
5  do  if a < 7
6       then tryrule(a) -> next;
7            if history matches [== ^next ==]
8            then a+1 -> a
9            else next -> current;
10                [^^history ^current] -> history;
11                1 -> a
12           endif
13      else history --> [== ?previous ^current ==];
14           previous -> current;
15           [^^history ^previous] -> history;
16           [backtracked] =>
17                1 -> a
18      endif
19 enduntil
20 history =>
21 enddefine;
```

This addition to the program completes the definition of depth. On line 5, the system checks to see whether a is less than 7, (i.e. are there any rules left to try). If so, the usual trying of the next rule takes place. Otherwise, on lines 13 to 17, current is assigned its previous value, this is added to history, the system then prints out [backtracked], a is assigned the value 1, and the whole process starts again. Line 16 is optional, but it sometimes helps to keep a track of what is going on inside a program by giving yourself messages as the program proceeds.

On line 20, after the whole process is complete, the variable history is printed. This will have the value of a list of states, representing steps to the solution.

Let's try the program out.

```
: dstartup();
: depth();
** [ [0 0] [4 0] [4 3] [0 3] [3 0] [3 3] [4 2] [0 2] [2 0] ]
```

It works!

So we have found a solution in eight steps to the jugs problem. In this solution no dead-ends have been encountered – as evidenced by the fact that we have not been informed of any backtracking.

One of the problems with a depth-first search is that it is very important in which order you try the rules. The ordering which we have imposed, in which filltap("x") is tried first, filltap("y") second and so on, is arbitrary; there is no real reason why the rules should be ordered like this. Depending on how you order the rules, you are going to get different solutions. Assuming that there is more than one way to reach the solution, different orderings of rules will lead you to different solutions first. To illustrate this, change the tryrule procedure so that the order of the rules is as follows:

```
afromb("x","y")
empty("y")
filltap("x")
empty("x")
afromb("y","x")
filltap("y")
```

You can do this by shuffling round the numbers or the procedure calls in tryrule.

Let's try the search procedure with this ordering:

```
: dstartup();
depth();
** [ [0 0] [4 0] [1 3] [1 0] [0 1] [4 1] [2 3] ]
```

This ordering gives us a quite different solution. This time the solution is reached in six steps, and once again, no dead-ends are encountered.

As well as changing the order of the rules, we could also tamper with other elements of the program, such as the start or goal states used. Let's change the starting state to [3 0], and see how this alters the behaviour of the program. To make this change, we can simply re-define dstartup:

```
define dstartup();
[3 0] -> current;
[^current] -> history;
enddefine;
```

If we use this starting state in conjunction with our re-ordered rules, the following solution is found:

```
: dstartup();
: depth();
** [backtracked]
** [backtracked]
** [backtracked]
** [ [3 0] [4 0] [0 0] [0 3] [4 3] [0 3] [0 0] [4 0] [1 3]
     [1 0] [0 1] [4 1] [2 3] ]
```

Here we have three backtracks, and again, a quite different solution. Looking at history you can see the route the program has taken. This is represented in Figure 7.8.

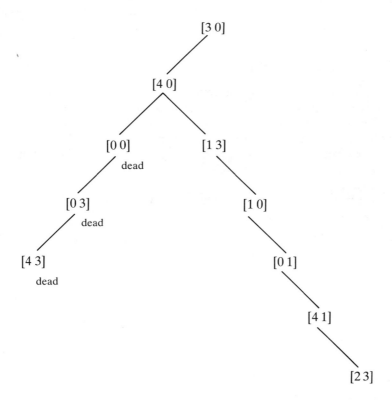

Figure 7.8 Changing the starting state alters the behaviour of the program.

You might like to write a program to operate on history so that the user receives only the direct path to the solution found, rather than a complete history of the paths tried.

Instead of changing all these parameters by hand as in this section, we could have written the program in more general terms in the first place. The start state, goal state, capacity of jugs and the ordering of the rules could all be written as variables in the program. You could then write a simple front-end to the program, asking the user for values for these variables. You could try this as an exercise. However, if you do, be warned: this program was written in the sure knowledge that the problem, as originally stated, has possible solutions. What would happen in the procedure depth if no solution was ever reached? Clearly, you need to add to depth so that it will stop when all possible paths have been tried – otherwise it will go on for ever. We will leave readers to discover a means of doing this themselves. However, as a hint, think about how many times you would have to backtrack all the way to the starting state, in order to be satisfied that you had exhausted the problem space.

In the next section we will build a program to implement a breadth-first search to solve the jugs problem.

7.3.4 Breadth-first search

The breadth-first search is going to look a little different from the depth-first search inasmuch as we now want to keep a record of lots of paths all at once. In this case we will keep a record of *paths* in the variable history, rather than keeping individual states as the elements of this list.

We will build up to this procedure by stages. Here is an outline of what we want the procedure to do:

UNTIL there is a path which ends with the goal state

DO for every path in the current history:

    (i) delete that path from the history

    (ii) try all rules in turn

        IF   the rule produces a state already in the path

        THEN do nothing

        ELSE add the state onto the end of the path
              and add the whole lot as an element
              to history

      ENDIF
ENDUNTIL

So when we are generating new paths from old ones, we first delete the old ones from history and then add all possible new ones. When there are no new paths possible from the state of an old one, the old one is dropped. For this reason, we have no problem with dead-ends in a breadth-first search – paths which lead to dead-ends just do not get considered further.

Before we write any code for this search, we need to initialize our states. In this case, we will not initialize a global variable current, as this will now correspond to the end state of any path – we will re-set it as we consider each new path. However, we will need to initialize history, a list containing lists of paths. In the first instance there is only one state, [0 0], and so we can define a startup program like this:

```
define bstartup();
[ [ [0 0] ] ] -> history;
enddefine;
```

So initially history has only one path in it. Furthermore, this path has only one element in it.

Now we will write the breadth program. It is quite possible to write this program as one procedure – however, it will make our lives easier to write two procedures here, so that we can easily read the program. The one-procedure solution is quite difficult to understand.

The first thing we need is a procedure which, given a path, will delete that path from history and add any new paths available from it to history, (i.e. a procedure to carry out part (ii) of the above English description of the program). We will then write a second procedure which applies part (i) of the description to all the paths in history. We shall call the first procedure gennext. Here is a definition:

```
1   define gennext(path);
2   vars a current next;
3   1 -> a;
4   path --> [== ?current];
5   delete(path,history) -> history;
6   until a > 6
7   do   tryrule(a) -> next;
8        if path matches [== ^next ==]
9        then
10       else [^^history [^^path ^next]] -> history
11       endif;
12       a+1 -> a
13  enduntil
14  enddefine;
```

On line 4, the procedure sets the variable current to have the value of the last state in the path under consideration.

On line 5, the built-in procedure delete is used. This procedure simply deletes an element from a list. Were it not already defined, we could very easily define it.

Lines 6 to 13 ensure that every rule is tried. For every rule which produces a novel state, the path followed by the state is added to the list history (on line 10).

We can now use this procedure in a definition of our searching procedure. This procedure, which we will call breadth, will perform the
'outer' part of the English description given above.

```
1   define breadth();
2   vars i oldhist fpath yend;
3   until history matches [ == [??fpath [2 ?yend]] ==]
4   do   history -> oldhist;
5       1 -> i;
6       until i > length(oldhist)
7       do  gennext(oldhist(i));
8           i+1 -> i
9       enduntil
10  enduntil;
11  [Shortest path is] =>
12  [^^fpath [2 ^yend]] =>
13  enddefine;
```

Line 3 represents the stopping condition. If a match is made, we pick
up the values of the rest of the path (fpath) and the contents of jug Y
(yend) in order to produce them as answers (lines 11 and 12).

On line 4 the present value of history is stored as another variable,
oldhist.

Lines 6 to 9 simply say, for every path in oldhist, do gennext. You can
now see why we needed to store the old value of history in a separate list
– history is constantly being changed by gennext and so we need to keep a
record of what it used to look like at the beginning of this run through the
rules.

Let's try running the procedure:

```
: bstartup();
: breadth();
** [Shortest path is]
** [[0 0] [4 0] [1 3] [1 0] [0 1] [4 1] [2 3]]
```

So the quickest solution to the problem takes six steps. If you want to see
all the states the program has considered, look at history:

```
: history ==>
** [[[0 0] [4 0] [4 3] [0 3] [3 0] [3 3] [4 2]]
   [[0 0] [4 0] [1 3] [4 3] [0 3] [3 0] [3 3]]
   [[0 0] [4 0] [1 3] [0 3] [3 0] [3 3] [4 3]]
   [[0 0] [4 0] [1 3] [0 3] [3 0] [3 3] [4 2]]
   [[0 0] [4 0] [1 3] [1 0] [0 1] [4 1] [4 3]]
   [[0 0] [4 0] [1 3] [1 0] [0 1] [4 1] [2 3]]
   [[0 0] [4 0] [1 3] [1 0] [0 1] [0 3] [4 3]]
   [[0 0] [4 0] [1 3] [1 0] [0 1] [0 3] [3 0]]
```

```
[[0 0] [0 3] [4 3] [4 0] [1 3] [1 0] [0 1]]
[[0 0] [0 3] [3 0] [4 0] [1 3] [1 0] [0 1]]
[[0 0] [0 3] [3 0] [3 3] [4 3] [4 0] [1 3]]
[[0 0] [0 3] [3 0] [3 3] [4 2] [4 3] [4 0]]
[[0 0] [0 3] [3 0] [3 3] [4 2] [0 2] [2 0]]
[[0 0] [0 3] [3 0] [3 3] [4 2] [4 0] [4 3]]
[[0 0] [0 3] [3 0] [3 3] [4 2] [4 0] [1 3]]]
```

You can see from this that there are two ways of reaching the solution in six steps. If you want to, you could draw out the explored problem space to see where the different branches were going.

It is evident from the history list that this method of searching has the disadvantage of having to carry around a lot of information (states) which will turn out to be redundant. In fact the representation of history used in this example is still more cumbersome than it need be, as some states are represented in every path. As an exercise, try to modify the program so that sequences of states used by more than one path are only represented once – i.e. use your history list to represent a hierarchy. You will need to think about how you will trace the path to your solution once you have reached it.

We have now finished writing POP-11 for this chapter. In the next section we will briefly consider some other search strategies but these will not be implemented as programs.

7.4 More search strategies

The strategies considered above are all very well for small problems. However, they are both a bit cumbersome, and can be just too inefficient for convenience in large problems. Consider, for example, the eights problem mentioned in Section 7.1. The slab can be in over sixteen thousand states. So a depth-first search for this problem would be very wasteful in exploring very long branches which eventually lead to dead-ends. A breadth-first search would have to carry around an enormous amount of information from step to step, and this would make the strategy very inefficient. There is a way of combining these two strategies to get a more efficient search through the problem space. This is called a **best-first** search.

7.4.1 Best-first search

A best-first search depends on being able to take some measurement of how close a particular state is to the goal state. The way of measuring this is called a **heuristic function**. A heuristic is a 'rule of thumb' used in solving problems. It is not a rigid specification for finding a solution, but a help along the way. The 'closeness' functions in a best-first search are called heuristic functions because they are often based on such rules of thumb. As an example, a heuristic function for the eights problem might be simply to count how many tiles are in the required position – the higher the number, the closer you are to a solution. It's a bit more difficult to think of a heuristic function for the water jugs problem.

Now if we can measure how close any state is to the goal, we can choose to follow the path which seems most promising. Here is a method for doing a best-first search.

1. Generate all possible states from the start state.

2. Apply the heuristic function to all states which have not been expanded and note how close they are to the goal.

3. If any states are the goal, you've finished. Otherwise choose the state nearest to the goal (whether this is a new state, or an old state which has not been expanded) and apply all the rules again to generate new states. Go back to (2).

Using this strategy, we can always make sure that the particular state which we are exploring is the nearest to the goal. As long as our heuristic function is a reasonable estimator of how close a state is to the goal state, this strategy will save us searching many redundant branches.

7.4.2 Backwards and non-linear search

All the search strategies considered so far have been characterized as **forwards** search strategies. This means that the search proceeds by starting at the start-state, and generating states until we reach a goal state. It is quite reasonable, however, to consider a **backwards** search strategy – one which begins at the goal, and applies all the rules in reverse until the start state is achieved. This is quite a common strategy in human problem solving. For example, when people try to solve problems like the water jugs they often start at the solution and ask themselves 'how could the jugs have got into this state?' rather than generating lots of new states from the initial one.

All the search strategies mentioned above could be employed in backwards reasoning. You might choose to employ backwards reasoning if the problem space gives rise to more start states than goal states, or if there are fewer branches emanating backwards from the goal than forward from the start. Examine the problem space for the water jugs problem (with a pencil and paper) and try to decide whether a backwards search might be a more efficient way to solve the problem (use a depth-first strategy). These issues will be discussed further in Chapter 9.

As well as backwards and forwards searches, there are also strategies which combine the two. These are called **non-linear** search strategies, and they can often provide a very powerful means of searching a problem space. One example of a non-linear strategy would be to start a forwards-reasoning and a backwards-reasoning search at the same time. We would then hope that the two searches would meet in the middle somewhere, by both finding themselves at the same state.

Another non-linear strategy is the technique of **means-ends analysis**. In this strategy the problem is broken up into big and small problems, and by choosing appropriate rules, you can then devise a search which solves the big problems first and then goes back to solve the small ones. Such an analysis is appropriate for more complex problems than those tackled here, and will be discussed in Chapter 9.

The topic of problem solving dealt with in this chapter is a common concern for very many workers in AI. There are many advanced texts on the topic and the interested student will want to follow these up. However, the purpose of this chapter has been to show you that POP-11 is a quite appropriate language in which to write problem solving programs.

In the next chapter we will look at another important area of AI – that of knowledge representation.

Chapter 8 **Knowledge Representation**

8.1 Introduction

In the last chapter we examined ways of solving the water jug problem. The domain for this problem is very small, and when we considered ways of representing the water jug world (page 90) we quickly decided that all the information needed about the current state of that world could be represented as a two-element list. However, many AI programs are written to operate on much larger and more complex domains. In these cases we have to face the issue of how we are going to represent the information in a way that is easy to use with the kinds of problems faced in that domain. This is the issue of knowledge representation.

In this chapter we start by building a POP-11 program to demonstrate one particular technique for knowledge representation. We then discuss two alternative techniques, providing a basic implementation for one of them. The technique discussed first relies on the idea of a **semantic net**.

A semantic net is essentially a set of nodes (usually items which you want to represent knowledge about) connected by a set of links (referred to as **arcs**). The arcs are labelled, and represent relationships between the nodes. Figure 8.1 is an example of a semantic net. From the network illustrated, we can retrieve simple items of information represented by two nodes and a connecting arc, such as George Eliot is the author of Middlemarch. Furthermore, we can deduce implicit information, such as the fact that Middlemarch is a book. The important thing to note here is that we do not have to include an explicit link between 'Middlemarch' and 'Book' in the net. (This example seems obvious to us because we understand that all novels are books, and that Middlemarch is a novel – the point is to represent this knowledge in a formal way.)

The idea of a semantic net is flexible enough to allow a variety of different ways of organizing information. In this chapter we shall build a semantic net in which nodes are organized as a hierarchy. For the purposes of our example we shall use a psychological domain. However, the issues in knowledge representation have a very wide range of applicability in both pure and applied research. Do not think that our example domain represents the be-all and end-all of knowledge representation. The same

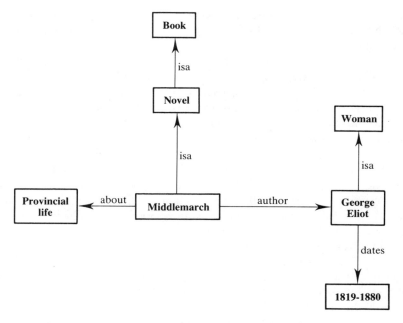

Figure 8.1 Example of a semantic net.

programming issues are just as likely to crop up in an automated banking system as in a model of human cognition.

One of the most difficult problems facing psychologists is the organization of semantic memory. Consider the problem for a moment. Semantic memory is that part of human memory which allows us to understand the *meaning* of concepts. Semantic memory is fundamental to explaining how we understand words in our language – since, of course, these words are representations of concepts. So we all know that a dog is an animal and a caterpiller is an animal but a bus is not an animal. But how do we store this information? Perhaps we have something in our heads which represents the concept 'bus', with all kinds of things linked to it; for example, 'is large', 'is often red', 'is not an animal' and so forth. However, this seems unlikely as there would have to be an almost indefinite number of links to each concept (for example, think how many 'is-not-a' links would have to be made to 'bus'). Psychologists interested in semantic memory are faced with the problem of constructing models which plausibly account for the way people understand the world.

One of the earliest attempts to tackle the problem of semantic memory was made by Collins and Quillian (1969). They proposed that semantic memory is organized in a hierarchical fashion, such that concepts on a given level are examples of a category on the level above, and have their own subordinate categories on the level below. Furthermore, each node has an associated set of characteristics which are shared by all its subordinates.

Such a representation can be modelled as a semantic net with two sorts of arc, 'isa' and 'hasproperty' arcs. Figure 8.2 shows such a hierarchy, representing part of our knowledge about the animal kingdom. The arcs linked to the tops and bottoms of nodes represent *isa* links, while those to the side represent *hasproperty* links. From this representation we can see that it is possible to infer that a spaniel is warm-blooded, because one of its superordinate nodes has that property. This will save a lot of storage space when we come to represent the information on a computer, as we do not have to include the property 'warm-blooded' as an associate of every mammal individually. This technique, a very common one in AI programs, is called **inheritance**, i.e. subordinate nodes inherit properties associated with their superordinates.

In the rest of this chapter we will build a representation of this hierarchy in POP-11. We shall also write procedures allowing us to explore the knowledge thus represented. For the purposes of this chapter we are only interested in problems of representing a model in POP-11, not in whether the model is good or bad psychologically. If you want to know more about the original semantic memory model, and alternatives to it, you should follow this up in a text on memory (e.g. Eysenck, 1984).

8.2 Representing the world

How are we going to represent the information present in Figure 8.2 as POP-11 code? We need some way of representing each node, along with its properties, and its subordinate nodes. Whenever we have a large amount of information, it is worth asking whether there is any way we can sensibly store it in the POP-11 database. If so, we will save a lot of time by using the pre-defined procedures available for use with the database.

In fact we can easily represent the information stored at each node as a list. The list representing this information must contain: the name of the node; the properties associated with the node; and the names of subordinate nodes. In order to use the database efficiently, we need to adopt a convention for representing this information. Let's adopt the following convention; each node is represented by a list of the following form:

```
[ NAME OF NODE [props ...] [subs ...] ]
```

Of course, there are many other possible conventions, but the important point is that we should be consistent. Given this, the above seems like a sensible format for representing the information stored at each node.

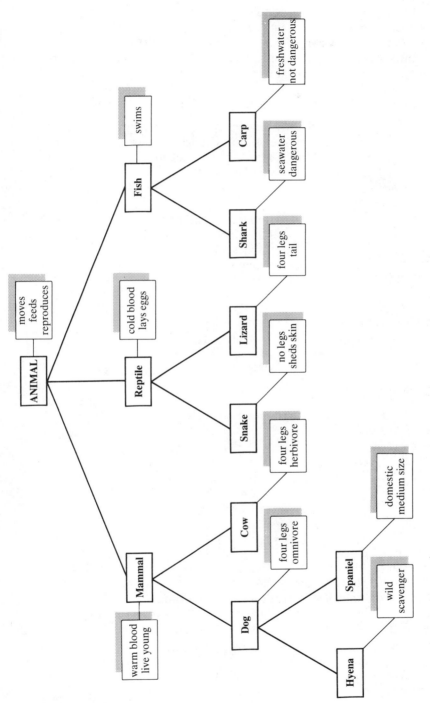

Figure 8.2 Hierarchical semantic net.

In fact we can think of this list (and hence each node) as being a structure with three **slots**, into which the three attributes associated with each node are put. For this reason such structures are often called **slot-and-filler** structures. Possibly a more obvious slot-and-filler representation for each node would be:

```
[[node [NAME OF NODE]] [props [PROPERTIES]] [subs [SUBORDINATES]]]
```

This makes it clearer that the network can be represented by sets of 3-slot elements. However, this seems a bit clumsy for our programs which will match the items (see below) so we will stick to the simpler format we introduced first. (As an exercise you might like to go through this chapter again once you have read it, and change the programs to operate on the second form.)

We will now write a procedure to initialize the database. Although we could add each list to the database separately at the start of each session, it will make life easier if we can simply execute a procedure whenever we want the database to contain the information given in Figure 8.2. We will call the procedure setup.

Here is a definition of setup:

```
define setup();
[] -> database;                    ;;; clear database initially
add([animal [props moves feeds reproduces]
                            [subs mammal reptile fish]]);
add([mammal [props warm_blood live_young] [subs dog cow]]);
add([reptile [props cold_blood lays_eggs] [subs lizard snake]]);
add([fish [props swims] [subs carp shark]]);
add([dog [props four_legs omnivore] [subs spaniel hyena]]);
add([cow [props four_legs herbivore] [subs]]);
add([lizard [props four_legs tail] [subs]]);
add([snake [props no_legs sheds_skin] [subs]]);
add([carp [props freshwater not_dangerous] [subs]]);
add([shark [props seawater dangerous] [subs]]);
add([spaniel [props domestic medium_size] [subs]]);
add([hyena [props wild scavenger] [subs]])
enddefine;
```

Notice that we keep the same format for all lists, even when this means including redundant information (e.g. even though "carp" is at the lowest level of the hierarchy, we include a "subs" list with no subordinates in it). This is because a standard format will make it easier to write programs which operate generally, on all lists.

If we execute this procedure we will have a representation of the animals hierarchy stored in the database. We now need to construct ways of getting information out of our store of knowledge.

8.3 Interrogating the world

Our semantic net has two different types of arc, i.e. two kinds of relationship. These are represented as 'isa' and 'props'. So we may write procedures which allow us to ask whether one node is a subcategory of another (i.e. whether there is a legitimate *isa* relationship between them) or whether a node has particular properties associated with it. Let us consider a procedure for the former problem first.

We will write a procedure which takes two arguments. If the first argument has the relationship *isa* to the second argument, the procedure will return <true>, otherwise it will return <false>. In the simplest case this will be a trivial exercise, as we will be able merely to examine the list beginning with the second argument and see whether the first argument is a subordinate of it (e.g. it will be easy to say that a "spaniel" is a "dog"). However, for more complex relationships where there is no list containing both arguments, we will have to make the program do some extra work (e.g. to establish that a "spaniel" is a "mammal"). This extra work, inferring knowledge which is not explicitly given, is an example of reasoning in a program.

We will build our procedure step by step, starting with the simplest possible version. Let's call it isa. Here is a first attempt at a definition:

```
define isa(lower,higher);
if present([^higher = [subs == ^lower == ]])
then true
else false
endif
enddefine;
```

We have called the arguments lower and higher in this procedure to remind us that the first argument represents the node lower in the hierarchy than the second argument. This procedure simply checks whether the lower argument is represented as a subcategory of the higher argument. So:

```
: isa("spaniel","dog") =>
** <true>
: isa("cow","reptile") =>
** <false>
: isa("spaniel","mammal") =>
** <false>
```

The procedure works for one *isa* arc only. We now have to write a procedure which will traverse more than one arc. In order to do this we could establish the name of the superordinate category to our lower argument and then check to see whether this is a subordinate of our higher argument. If not, we could find the superordinate of the superordinate and so on. Here is a revised version of the procedure working on this principle. The lines are numbered for easy reference:

```
1 define isa(lower,higher);
2 vars nextup;
3 if present([^higher = [subs == ^lower == ]])
4 then true
5 else lookup([?nextup = [subs == ^lower == ]]);
6       isa(nextup,higher)
7 endif
8 enddefine;
```

Try this procedure with some example arguments, which you would expect to return <true>.

```
: isa("spaniel","dog") =>
** <true>
: isa("spaniel","mammal") =>
** <true>
: isa("spaniel","animal") =>
** <true>
: isa("dog","animal") =>
** <true>
```

How does this procedure work? Let's talk through it with the example

```
isa("spaniel","animal") =>
```

On line 3, the procedure looks to see whether there is a list in the database beginning with "animal" which includes "spaniel" as a subordinate. As no such list exists the system next considers line 5. Here, a list is found such that "spaniel" is a subordinate of something, and this something ("dog" in this case) is assigned to the variable nextup. On line 6, the procedure isa is called recursively with arguments "dog" and "animal". Once again, the conditional on line 3 is false and so on line 5, the superordinate of "dog" (i.e. "mammal") is assigned to nextup and the procedure isa is called with argument "mammal" and "animal". This time, the conditional in line 3 is true, and so the procedure returns <true> and terminates.

So this procedure does not need to be told how many steps to take in search of a connection; it simply keeps looking further and further up the hierarchy until it finds a category in a path above the lower argument, which is immediately below the higher argument. However, there is a problem. What happens when there is no such connection? Try the following:

```
: isa("cow","reptile") =>
MISHAP ...
```

The procedure does not seem to be able to deal with arguments which should make it return <false>. This is hardly surprising as we have provided the procedure with no apparatus to return <false>. To find out where the procedure fails in this situation we could trace it in operation:

```
: trace isa;
: isa("cow","reptile") =>

> isa cow reptile
!> isa mammal reptile
!!> isa animal reptile
MISHAP ...
```

This tells us that the procedure fails once it has worked all the way up the hierarchy from "cow" to "animal". In fact the procedure produces a MISHAP when trying to perform:

```
lookup([?nextup = [subs == animal ==]]);
```

Remember that lookup produces an error when there is no list in the database matching its argument. So we need to include a stopping condition in our procedure in order to avoid this MISHAP and to return <false> if we have searched all legal connections. This stopping condition will tell the procedure that it is to stop if there is nowhere higher to go than the current lower argument. Here is the final version of the procedure:

```
1 define isa(lower,higher);
2 vars nextup;
3 if present([^higher = [subs == ^lower == ]])
4 then true
5 elseif present([?nextup = [subs == ^lower == ]]);
6 then isa(nextup,higher)
7 else false
8 endif
9 enddefine;
```

We can avoid the problems with MISHAPs if we use present instead of lookup. Remember that lookup causes a MISHAP if the pattern is not found, whereas present returns <false> if the pattern is not found. The above procedure works in the same way as the previous definition except that it allows for the possibility that there is no category higher than the current value of lower. If there is no such list present (as checked on line 5) the system goes to line 7 and returns <false>. In our world, the only node which does not have a superordinate category is the node called "animals". So if this procedure has checked all the nodes between lower and higher (including "animals") then it must return <false> as there is nowhere left to look. Try this procedure with a few example arguments. If you trace the procedure you will be able to observe that it only returns <false> if all the possible *isa* links between lower and "animal" have been tried.

Of course the procedure is not yet foolproof. Whenever you write a procedure you need to make a decision about what it is going to be able to handle (see page 46). In this case, we have decided not to give the procedure power to treat unrecognized nodes in any unique way. For example:

```
: isa("horse","mammal") =>
** <false>
```

We would expect to get a <false> value returned here, as there is no reference to "horse" in the database. However, it might be more appropriate for the procedures to distinguish between those instances where it can prove a false link (e.g. isa("shark","mammal")), and those where it does not have any knowledge about the arguments supplied. As an exercise, you could extend isa to cope with arguments which are not present in the database. Such an extension would check for the presence of arguments in the database and print an appropriate message if they are not to be found.

Having written a working isa procedure, it is now quite trivial to write a hasprop procedure to check whether an animal has a certain property. Given that we have been consistent in the form of our database lists, we need only change isa slightly in order to write a working hasprop procedure. Here is such a procedure. Its first argument creature, refers to the animal in question, and its second argument property refers to the property we wish to check for.

```
1 define hasprop(creature,property);
2 vars nextlevel;
3 if present([^creature [props == ^property ==] = ])
4 then true
5 elseif present([?nextlevel = [subs == ^creature ==]])
6 then hasprop(nextlevel,property)
7 else false
8 endif
9 enddefine;
```

The only difference between the two procedures is that we are now looking at a different part of a database item. This is evident by the template given to present on line 3.

Let's try this procedure:

```
: hasprop("snake","no_legs") =>
** <true>

: hasprop("dog","live_young") =>
** <true>
```

```
: hasprop("hyena","feeds") =>
** <true>

: hasprop("carp","live_young") =>
** <false>
```

Now there are various other things we might want to know about this knowledge base of ours. For more practice in dealing with semantic nets we will write one further program for interrogating the hierarchy of animals.

The original conception of a hierarchical semantic memory structure makes certain predictions depending on how far apart nodes are in the network, i.e. how many *isa* arcs you have to traverse in order to get from one node to another. So, for example, we can say that "spaniel" and "dog" are 1 arc apart, whereas "hyena" and "cow" are 3 arcs apart (2 down from "mammal" to "hyena", and 1 from "mammal" to "cow"). Specifically, it was hypothesized that people would take longer to decide on the truth or falsity of distant relationships (e.g. a hyena is a mammal) than on closer relationships (e.g. a spaniel is a dog). Furthermore, some psychologists hypothesized that for a time after one had entered the network at a particular node, neighbouring nodes would be more easily accessible. So, for example, if a person had just seen the word 'dog', then it would be easier for them to recognize the word 'cow' than the word 'snake', as the former is closer to the original in the network. This is called the hypothesis of **semantic priming**. If we wanted to write a program to model this conception and test the predictions, we would need some way of measuring distance between nodes. This will be the function of the next program.

The problem can be stated as follows: given any two nodes in the hierarchy, what is the smallest number of *isa* arcs which we need to traverse in order to link them? One way to tackle the problem is this:

1. For each of the two nodes, generate a list of all nodes between it and the highest level (include the original node).
2. Find the first element which appears in both lists.
3. Count the number of elements appearing in each list before the first common element and add these two numbers together.

To convince you that this algorithm works, here is an example applying to "hyena" and "cow" which we have already agreed are 3 arcs apart.

Step 1   gives a list of [hyena dog mammal animal] for the "hyena" node; and [cow mammal animal] for the "cow" node.

Step 2   gives the first common element "mammal".

Step 3   gives 2 + 1 = 3.

A more obvious way to go about this would be to join the fronts of the two lists given by step 1, with the first common superordinate category in the middle. In this example we would end up with [hyena dog mammal cow]. We could then count the steps between the elements – i.e. the length of the list minus one. However, this always gives the same answer as the above algorithm, and involves more computational steps. Therefore we will stick to the original for the purposes of our program.

The first procedure we need is one which will make a list of all the nodes superordinate to a given node. Here is such a procedure:

```
1 define allabove(node);
2 vars sups;
3 [^node] -> sups;
4 while present([?nextup = [subs == ^node ==]])
5 do  [^^sups ^nextup] -> sups;
6     nextup -> node
7 endwhile;
8 sups
9 enddefine;
```

This procedure is based on a similar principle to that governing the isa and hasprop procedures defined above, the difference being that allabove uses iterative rather than recursive techniques. On line 3 we initialize the local variable sups to have the value of the node, put in a list. Lines 4 to 7 then ensure that as long as there is a node above the current one, it is added to the list sups, and the superordinate node becomes the current one. On line 8 the final version of sups is left on the stack. So,

```
: allabove("hyena") =>
** [hyena dog mammal animal]

: allabove("cow") =>
** [cow mammal animal]
```

We now need a procedure to perform step 2 of the algorithm. In fact, we wrote a procedure to find a common element in two lists in Chapter 4. Here is another such definition:

```
define inboth(list1,list2);
if list1 = []
then false
elseif list2 matches [== ^(hd(list1)) ==]
then hd(list1)
else inboth(tl(list1),list2)
endif
enddefine;
```

(In Chapter 4 we had not introduced matching notation and so the definition of isinboth on page 47 requires access to another procedure.) If you cannot see how the procedure inboth works, you should go back and re-read the explanation of isinboth given in Chapter 4.

We can now use the two procedures defined above in a very simple final procedure to perform step 3 of the algorithm. We will call this procedure distance. Here is a definition.

```
1 define distance(node1,node2);
2 vars sups1 sups2 common front1 front2;
3 allabove(node1) -> sups1;
4 allabove(node2) -> sups2;
5 inboth(sups1,sups2) -> common;
6 sups1 --> [??front1 ^common ==];
7 sups2 --> [??front2 ^common ==];
8 length(front1)+length(front2)
9 enddefine;
```

Having generated the nodes above each argument (lines 3 and 4), line 5 simply calls inboth to find the common element. On lines 6 and 7 variables front1 and front2 are assigned the value of the list of elements preceding the common element. On line 8 these elements are counted, summed, and the results left on the stack. Let's try this procedure:

```
: distance("hyena","cow") =>
** 3

: distance("dog","shark") =>
** 4

: distance("snake","reptile") =>
** 1

: distance("carp","carp") =>
** 0
```

The procedure seems to work. As an exercise, try to alter the distance procedure so that it prints out the node at which the two paths meet, as well as the distance between them. For example, "hyena" and "cow" meet at "mammal". You should be able to do this by adding one line to distance.

At this point, we will stop adding to our programs to explore the semantic net. Of course, there are many ways in which the example could be extended, and you might like to do so yourself. However, the important aspects of the net have now been covered, and further additions would not illustrate any new ideas.

Before we go on to discuss other techniques in knowledge representation, it is worth making one general point. Knowledge representation is not concerned solely with the way you choose to store your data (i.e. how we chose to structure the database in our animals example). In fact, it is necessary to talk about that data *in conjunction with* the methods of reasoning associated with it. Once we have structured our database, we cannot say that we have represented any knowledge at all – the information in it only becomes a representation of knowledge when we build procedures to explore and utilize it. To see this, think about a telephone directory. A telephone directory is not a representation of knowledge itself – it only becomes so when we understand how it is organized, i.e. when we develop or are taught methods of finding out information from it.

This point is general to (almost) all techniques for knowledge representation, as we shall see in the next section. In short, we could characterize the issue with the slogan:

Knowledge representation = data + reasoning.

8.4 Other knowledge representation techniques

The issue of knowledge representation is currently attracting a great deal of interest in AI research. In fact there are myriad techniques available, and the researcher must decide which best suites the requirements of the domain. In this section we will provide a brief account of two common techniques. The reader seriously interested in the issues should look elsewhere for a more detailed account of the field (e.g. Charniak and McDermot, 1985).

Before we describe particular techniques, one word of warning: when considering how to implement a particular knowledge representation scheme in POP-11, ask yourself whether the actual program will look any different from one based on another scheme. It is sometimes the case that arguments about knowledge representation techniques are merely arguments about the way in which to describe the same thing. If the program turns out to look the same under two different techniques, you should be suspicious of any distinction drawn between the two.

8.4.1 Logic

The use of logic as a tool for knowledge representation has been popular in AI, particularly in selected domains of study. The most popular technique relies on utilizing a traditional logic called **predicate calculus**. A predicate is a relation between a set of arguments – this relation is either true of these arguments or false. As an example, consider the predicate 'is_living'. When this is applied to the argument 'grass' the statement formed from the predicate and argument is TRUE, whereas if it is applied to 'rock' the statement is FALSE. Within predicate calculus the conventional way to represent the statement 'grass is living' is:

is_living(grass)

Don't be confused by the notation here. The convention looks like POP-11, but that is just coincidence; the above is an example of a statement in predicate calculus, not a statement in POP-11.

Examples of more complex logical statements might be

fatherof(Philip, Charles)
brotherof(Charles, Edward)

The predicates in these statements require two arguments. The statements could be read as: 'Philip is the father of Charles' and 'Charles is the brother of Edward'. Once again, such statements always evaluate to TRUE or FALSE.

Now logic provides us with its own set of ways to combine statements. These are called **connectives**. The five most commonly used are

And $\wedge$
Or $\vee$
Not $\neg$
Implies $\supset$
Equivalent $\equiv$

Using these connectives, we can form complex expressions like:

fatherof(Philip, Charles)$\wedge$brotherof(Charles, Edward)

which, as a whole evaluates to TRUE. Or,

fatherof(Philip, Charles)$\wedge$is_living(rock)

which, as a whole evaluates to FALSE.

There are two more symbols of importance in predicate logic which you need to know before you can use it in interesting ways. These are called **quantifiers**. The first, $\forall$, means 'for all ...', the second, $\exists$, means 'there exists a ...'. Consider the following statement in predicate logic:

$\forall X, Y$ brotherof$(X, Y) \supset$ brotherof(Y, X)

This reads: for all Xs and Ys, brotherof(X, Y) implies brotherof(Y, X). Using this scheme we can represent general rules, which apply to any arguments. Here is another example:

$\forall X,$ human$(X) \supset \exists Y,$ fatherof(Y, X)

or, in natural language, for all Xs who are human, there is a Y, such that Y is the father of X. Of course, what this boils down to is a logical statement of the rule 'everyone has a father'.

Once we have represented our domain in these terms, the reasoning powers available are defined by the facilities of logic. In fact, reasoning with the knowledge becomes equivalent to trying to prove statements in logic. So, for example, say we had a set of facts concerning family relations, along with a set of rules about such relations, we could then find out who is the uncle of Charles (say) by attempting to prove that

$\exists X,$ uncleof$(X,$ Charles$)$

is a true statement and, at the same time, finding the value of X for which
it is true. (You might think about how you could specify a predicate for
'uncleof' using 'fatherof' and 'brotherof'.)

This technique for knowledge representation is made very easy in a
different programming language called PROLOG, which forms part of the
POPLOG system (see Chapter 11). Those interested in the technique
might benefit from reading about PROLOG independently. However, it
is quite possible to represent logical expressions in POP-11 in a number of
ways. One way would be to represent the true statements in a database as
a set of lists, e.g.

```
[

    [fatherof [Philip Charles]]
    [fatherof [Charles Harold]]
    [brotherof [Charles Edward]]

        .
        .
        .

] -> database;
```

Complex rules could then be represented as procedures. We shall leave
this possibility open as an exercise to interested readers.

The purpose of this section has not been to show you how to represent
knowledge in logic, but simply to alert you to the possibility of doing so.
We shall now move on to another technique in knowledge representation.

8.4.2 Production systems

The final technique we describe for knowledge representation can be sum-
marized by the slogan 'knowledge as rules'. This technique has recently
become very important, as it is commonly used in the building of 'expert
systems'. These are programs which work on real-world problems which
may not be fully described with the neat, but constrained, techniques
which we have looked at so far. Examples of domains for which expert
systems have been built are: medical diagnosis of certain illnesses (Shortliffe, 1976); decisions about where to drill for certain mineral exploration
(Duda *et al.*, 1979); and advice about fault finding in complex electric
circuits (Stallman and Sussman, 1979). As you can imagine, these
domains do not readily lend themselves to a quick and easy description –
it takes people years of study and experience in order to become proficient
at these tasks. When trying to build a program to behave as an expert in
these fields, one needs a method of representing the knowledge in a flexible and modifiable way. As we will see in the rest of this chapter, production systems provide such a technique. In what follows, we do not construct an expert system (except of the most basic kind). However, we do
develop a small production system and show how it can be used.

A production system comprises three important parts: a set of production rules; a working memory; and a production system interpreter. Production rules are condition/action pairs which read as follows:

IF ⟨condition⟩ THEN ⟨action⟩

The left hand side, or condition, part of these rules usually refers to the presence or absence of some element (or set of elements) in the working memory. The action part usually performs some action on the working memory (adding or deleting elements) but might also include instructions to print information or stop the system running. The working memory (or 'context') can be thought of as a store of all the things currently known about the world – at its simplest, just a list of things which are known at any one time.

The interpreter is the program which makes decisions about which rules to use. If the left hand side (LHS) of a rule is satisfied, then the rule can be said to 'fire', i.e. to perform the actions in the right hand side (RHS). However, there are many possible ways of making the decision about which rules to fire, e.g. should all firable rules be made to fire or only one; if only one, which one; and so on. To illustrate these ideas we will write a program to demonstrate the workings of a very simple production system. We will return to more general issues, and more realistic uses of production systems at the end of this section.

Let us choose the domain of cooking a steak for our example. We will build a production system which gives instructions to a novice cook. We represent knowledge about steak cooking as a set of rules. Before we construct the rules, we need to be clear about what form they will take – decisions made at this stage will of course affect the construction of the interpreter program. Let's set up some constraints:

1. Working memory will simply be a list of elements.

2. The LHS of the rules will contain only one condition. This will require that an element is either in, or not in the working memory.

3. The RHS of the rules may contain any number of actions. The actions may only take three forms: (i) an instruction to print information; (ii) an instruction to add an element to working memory; (iii) an instruction to stop firing rules.

4. The interpreter will work as follows: all the rules will be examined, and all firable rules fired. This will alter the working memory. The process is then repeated. This goes on until a rule is fired whose action specifies that the process should stop.

All these constraints are artificial and in more interesting production systems (PSs) there will be much more flexibility. However, for the sake of this example, we need to make clear exactly what restrictions apply.

We will represent the various possible conditions and actions in the following way:

notin X	X is not in working memory
in X	X is in working memory
instruct X	print X
putin X	put X in working memory
stop X	stop firing rules

Here are six rules for cooking a steak using these relations:

1. IF notin have steak THEN instruct buy steak
             AND putin have steak.

2. IF in want to fry THEN instruct melt butter in pan
             AND instruct fry for 6 minutes
             AND putin frying.

3. IF in want to grill THEN instruct put under grill for 5 minutes
             AND putin grilling.

4. IF notin want to grill THEN putin want to fry.

5. IF in frying THEN instruct keep on hot plate
             AND instruct fry mushrooms in the butter
             AND instruct serve with mushrooms
             AND stop.

6. IF in grilling THEN instruct serve with a salad
             AND stop.

How are we going to represent these rules in POP-11? As usual there are many possible ways, but a reasonable one seems to be to represent each rule as a list in the database. Each list (i.e. rule) will have two elements, representing the LHS and RHS of the rule. As the RHS may contain several actions, it would be as well for it to be a list of lists, each embedded list representing one action. Here is a POP-11 representation:

```
[
    [ [notin have steak]    [[instruct buy steak]
                             [putin have steak]] ]
    [ [in want to fry]      [[instruct melt butter in pan]
                             [instruct fry for 6 minutes]
                             [putin frying]] ]
    [ [in want to grill]    [[instruct put under grill for 5 mins]
                             [putin grilling]] ]
    [ [notin want to grill] [[putin want to fry]] ]
    [ [in frying]           [[instruct keep on hot plate]
                             [instruct fry mushrooms in butter]
                             [instruct serve together]
                             [stop]] ]
```

```
    [ [in grilling]          [[instruct serve with salad]
                              [stop]] ]
] -> database;
```

As our working memory is simply to be a list, we can represent it as a global variable:

```
vars context;
[] -> context;
```

We must be sure to initialize this variable before each call of the PS.

We now have to build the interpreter. Here is an outline for the program:

```
1 define interpreter();
2 until TOLD TO STOP
3 do   foreach [?l ?r]
4       do  if CONDITION l IS TRUE
5            then DO ACTION r
6            endif
7        endforeach
8 enduntil
9 enddefine;
```

Lines 3 to 7 of this prototype procedure say: for each list in the database, assign the first element to the variable l, and the second to the variable r; if CONDITION l is satisfied, DO the ACTIONs specified in r.

We can see from this that we need to write two more procedures: one which will check whether a condition is true, and one which will perform a set of actions. We will call these procedures lhs and rhs. Here is a definition of lhs:

```
define lhs(cond);
vars spec item;
cond --> [?spec ??item];
if spec = "in"
then if context matches [== ^item ==]
     then true
     else false
     endif
elseif spec = "notin"
then if context matches [== ^item ==]
     then false
     else true
     endif
endif
enddefine;
```

Now this is not a very efficient way to write the procedure – you may like to think about how it could be written in half the number of lines. However, its structure does make it easy to read. Quite simply, if the first element of a condition is "in" then the rest must be in the context list for the procedure to return <true>. The opposite applies if the first element is "notin".

We now define rhs. Remember that the right hand sides of our rules are lists of lists – there may be many actions to perform. For this reason we will first write a procedure which applies one action, and then a procedure which applies it as many times as necessary. Here is the procedure for an action:

```
define obeyact(list);
vars x;
if list matches [instruct ??x]
then x =>
elseif list matches [putin ??x]
then [^x ^^context] -> context
elseif list = [stop]
then true -> stopper
endif
enddefine;
```

This procedure reflects the fact that our system only allows three actions: instruct (i.e. printing messages); putin (adding elements to the context list); and stop. The action indicated by the stop instruction is to set a variable to <true>. This will be used in our top level procedure.

It is now a simple matter to write a procedure to apply this procedure to a list of actions:

```
define rhs(acts);
until acts = []
do   obeyact(hd(acts));
     tl(acts) -> acts
enduntil
enddefine;
```

We can now write our interpreter program:

```
define interpreter();
vars l r stopper;
false -> stopper;
until stopper
do   foreach [?l ?r]
     do  if lhs(l)
         then rhs(r)
         endif
```

```
      endforeach
   enduntil
   enddefine;
```

This definition is not greatly different from our prototype definition. The only real addition is that we can now see how the stopping condition works – the interpreter continues to pass through the rules until the variable stopper is <true>.

Now let's see the procedure working. In the first instance we will initialize the context as empty:

```
: [] -> context;
: interpreter();
** [buy steak]
** [melt butter in pan]
** [fry for 6 minutes]
** [keep on hot plate]
** [fry mushrooms in butter]
** [serve together]
```

Let's see what happens when we start with different values in the working memory:

```
: [[want to grill]] -> context;
: interpreter();
** [buy steak]
** [put under grill for 5 mins]
** [serve with salad]

: [[have steak] [want to fry]] -> context;
: interpreter();
** [melt butter in pan]
** [fry for 6 minutes]
** [keep on hot plate]
** [fry mushrooms in butter]
** [serve together]
```

So, the production system seems to work.

Now this is clearly not a very sophisticated system. One obvious fault is that duplicative actions are allowed to occur (e.g. if you look at the list context now you will find that [want to fry] appears twice). However, it should give you a feel for representing knowledge as rules. As an exercise, you could use the above interpreter on a different set of rules – think of an example problem domain and then try to write some appropriate rules.

More sophisticated PSs typically have much more complex rules, for example the LHS of a rule might contain several conditions, linked by

AND and OR conditions. Furthermore, most systems do not fire every firable rule on each pass through the rule-set. That leaves the problem of how to decide which rule to fire when many are available. This issue is called 'conflict resolution' and has attracted a great deal of attention from AI programmers. One simple conflict resolution strategy involves simply ordering the rule-set by importance. The interpreter then fires the first applicable rule it comes to on each pass through the rule-set. Other strategies involve placing numerical values on each rule and applying mathematical criteria to the decision.

The main advantage of PSs, and the feature which makes them an attractive technique for expert systems is that each item of knowledge is individually accessible. You can easily add new rules or delete old ones. Furthermore, you can experiment with speculative rules without having to make any changes to the interpreter at all. When large rule-sets are needed (which they usually are in real applications) one often finds that the addition or deletion of a single rule will radically affect the behaviour of the system. Such easy encoding of knowledge is ideal for the real-world applications typically tackled in expert systems projects.

In this chapter we have considered three knowledge representation techniques. Of course there are many more, and the interested reader might look to a more advanced text for a detailed account of other popular techniques. In fact, knowledge representation is not really an isolated topic in AI – all knowledge based programs employ some form of knowledge representation. So whenever you write a program you will have to confront some of the issues raised in this chapter. This will be evident in Chapter 9, in which we discuss the idea of planning in AI.

Chapter 9 Goal Directed Behaviour: an Introduction to Planning

9.1 Backwards reasoning

In Chapter 7 we discussed some problem solving techniques within AI. The problems to which these techniques have been applied include the Tower of Hanoi problem, the eights puzzle and problems in algebra. These problems have a number of desirable properties from the viewpoint of the person trying to write programs to solve them. They have a definite starting state and a well defined solution – that is, we know what counts as a beginning and an end to such problems. They also have clear rules and constraints about ways in which the elements of the problem can be transformed.

We noted that these types of problem can seem rather contrived. Certainly they do not typify the kinds of problem we face in our daily lives. How does Patrick finish the chapter he has promised, get his next lecture prepared, be available to see students and convince the Prof. to give him a rise? These types of problem do not have all of the desirable properties of our formal problems. This is not to say that problem solving techniques are completely restricted to formal problems. Later in this chapter we shall be looking at a technique which, its proponents argue, is applicable to a broad range of problems. We shall begin the chapter by considering a different style of problem solving to that introduced in Chapter 7 – although the type of problem to which it is applied has a well defined formal structure and involves a micro-world. Within AI, the term 'micro-world' denotes a domain in which there are relatively few objects with simple properties, the world is subject to well defined transformations.

9.1.1 State space representations

In Chapter 7 we introduced the concept of state space representations. Such representations use two sorts of entity – states and operations. States are represented by data structures which record the condition of the problem elements at each stage in its solution. Operations are the means of transforming one state to another.

The initial state of the Tower of Hanoi problem is represented graphically in Figure 9.1.

Figure 9.1 Initial state of the Tower of Hanoi problem.

Within POP-11 such states could be represented in many different ways. An obvious representation is to use a list structure such as:

```
: vars state;
: [ [peg_a [3 2 1]] [peg_b [ ]] [peg_c [ ]] ] -> state;
```

This is a three-element list, each element of which is a list. These embedded lists consist of two elements – the name of the peg and a list of the rings on that peg. The order of the rings is interpreted by us as follows: left to right is bottom to top (an empty list is a peg with no rings on it).

When we consider the operations that can apply in this problem, the most general rule is that of moving a ring x from one peg y to another peg z. The constraints are that the ring must be exposed and not moved to cover a smaller ring.

Applying this general rule to an initial state in all legal ways allows us to grow a structure known as a **state space**. One way of representing this state space is to use an **OR tree**. Figure 9.2 represents part of the state space for the Hanoi problem represented in an OR tree. Each directed arc from a state represents the application of an operator to transform that state. Arcs leading from a particular state are viewed as alternatives to one another. This is how the OR tree gets its name.

When trying to solve a problem using state space representations we would like to explore as little of this structure as possible to find a solution. The part of the state space actually searched is known as the **search tree**.

We have already met breadth-first searching. A breadth-first search of our Hanoi state space would grow a search tree such as illustrated in Figure 9.3. Remember that the search algorithm disallows the generation of any state previously encountered. This can account for much of the computational work done in search. However, it does mean that at two

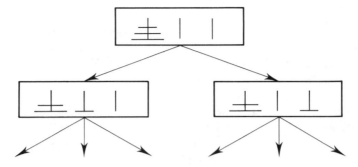

Figure 9.2 An OR tree can be used to represent a state space.

moves into the problem the only states generated in a breadth-first search are those shown in Figure 9.3.

We also mentioned in Chapter 7 that a search algorithm could be run on a state space so as to start from the initial state, and search forward to the goal state. This is known as **forward** search. We can also arrange for the algorithm to start with the goal state and search backwards for the initial state. This is **backwards** search. Both types of search rely on operators which generate exactly one new state from a predecessor state. Backwards search is sometimes called **goal directed** search. However, it is goal directed in a rather uninteresting sense.

There is a different kind of problem solving representation which uses the concept of goal directed backward reasoning in a more powerful way. We shall look at this in the next section.

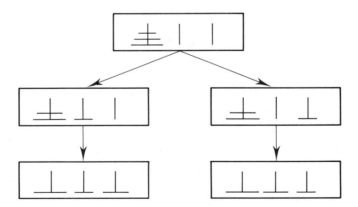

Figure 9.3 A search tree representing the first two moves of a breadth-first search for the Tower of Hanoi problem.

9.1.2 Problem reduction

In problem reduction an initial problem description is provided – this is the goal to be achieved. The goal is achieved by a sequence of operators which change the problem description into a set of sub-problems whose solutions are immediate. Operators in this representation have the property of producing a conjunction of new descriptions, each of which is a substantially simpler problem to solve than its predecessor. Goals or problems that are immediately soluble are known as primitive problems. Reasoning proceeds backwards from the original problem description and attempts to find a set of primitive problems whose solutions jointly solve the original problem.

We can represent this type of problem reduction using a structure known as an **AND/OR tree**. In an AND/OR tree the problem to be solved is the topmost node. The application of a problem reduction operator produces a set of arcs leading to sub-problems that must be jointly solved. These arcs are represented as AND conditions by a bar which joins them. In Figure 9.4a we see that problem 1 is solved by applying an operator which produces three sub-problems. These must be jointly solved. It is

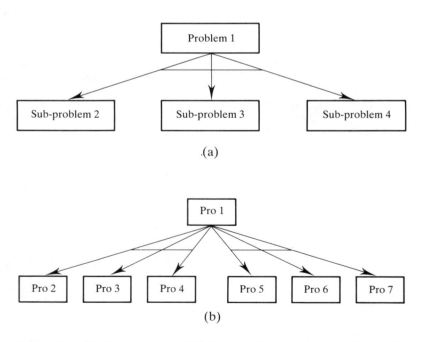

Figure 9.4 (a) An operator applied to problem 1 produces three sub-problems. (b) Two operators applied to problem 1 produce two different sets of sub-problems.

important to realize that we are not generating state spaces in this kind of representation. Each node represents a *problem* to be solved and is not a description of a state of affairs. Similarly the operators are operators that break problems up into smaller problems; they are not operations to transform one state of affairs in the world into another, rather they should be understood as *instructions* to perform such operations. A subtle but important conceptual difference, since this difference separates out the area of **planning** from other areas in AI. We can regard planning as the construction of a sequence of operations which are proposed by a system, a sequence which *if performed* attempts to bring about a desired goal state.

In Figure 9.4b we see that there are two operators which reduce 'pro1' to two different sets of sub-problems. We may solve problem 1 either by jointly solving problems 2, 3 and 4, or by jointly solving problems 5, 6 and 7. We have used both OR and AND arcs to represent a space of possible goals, the trees indicate which combinations of these goals will jointly satisfy the top level goal.

The Hanoi problem lends itself to problem reduction very nicely because there exists a powerful problem reduction operator which can be used. This operator is a rather clever way of breaking up the problem recursively into sub-components which will ultimately result in primitive problems. The operator is not one that we would expect to occur immediately to you as you performed such as task!

The operator can be expressed as follows:

With three pegs, a, b and c, to move n rings from peg a to peg c, solve the sub-problems:

1. Move the top $n-1$ rings from a to b.
2. Move the exposed ring from a to c.
3. Move the top $n-1$ rings from b to c.

The only primitive problem is to move a single exposed disk from one peg to another.

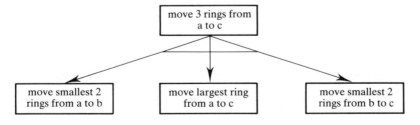

Figure 9.5 An AND/OR tree representation of the Tower of Hanoi problem.

A three-ring Hanoi problem with its relevant operator is represented in the AND/OR tree shown in Figure 9.5. Notice that this problem space provides no OR arcs. The operator provides a complete specification of how to solve the problem. Each node is a description of a problem to be solved – notice that the world is not represented explicitly but only in terms of the problems to be solved.

A search of this type of problem space is reasonably simple. We now look at some POP-11 procedures to do just this.

We can provide an initial problem description by specifying:

1. how many rings to be moved,
2. which peg they are on at the outset,
3. which the target peg is,
4. which peg can be used as a store.

This description can be represented in POP-11 as arguments to a procedure that will then apply the problem reduction operator. Our procedure is called solve_it and is defined below.

```
define solve_it(num_rings,initial_peg,target_peg,store_peg);
if num_rings = 1
then prim_prob(initial_peg,target_peg)
else ppr([Attempting to solve problem of moving ^num_rings]);nl(1);
     ppr([uppermost rings from ^initial_peg to ^target_peg]);nl(2);
     p_reduction(num_rings,initial_peg,target_peg,store_peg)
endif
enddefine;
```

The solve_it procedure first determines whether the arguments describe a one-ring problem. A one-ring problem can be solved by the primitive problem procedure prim_prob which we shall define below. If we are not dealing with a primitive problem, the procedure prints some information about the problem and then calls the problem reduction procedure p_reduction. This latter procedure is the one which will implement the problem reduction operator shown above. We shall define it shortly.

The definition of prim_prob is straightforward:

```
define prim_prob(i,t);
ppr([PRIMITIVE move exposed ring from ^i to ^t]); nl(2)
enddefine;
```

The output from prim_prob simply tells you to move the exposed ring from the initial peg to the target peg. This is an obvious solution for a one-ring problem. So if solve_it were called with the following arguments then we would observe:

```
: solve_it(1,"pega","pegc","pegb");
  PRIMITIVE move exposed ring from pega to pegc
```

We now turn to the definition of the problem reduction procedure. This is simply going to be a POP-11 version of the problem reduction operator. We can define it like this:

```
define p_reduction(nr, initial, target, store);
solve_it(nr-1, initial, store, target);
solve_it(1, initial, target, store);
solve_it(nr-1, store, target, initial)
enddefine;
```

This procedure implements our problem reduction operator by calling solve_it on three sub-problems. We can now see that solve_it is a recursive procedure. When solve_it calls p_reduction, it is in fact calling itself.

Let us examine the output of this program for a three-ring problem. We have numbered the chunks of output to help explain the program's behaviour:

```
: solve_it(3,"pega","pegc","pegb");
```

Attempting to solve the problem of moving 3 uppermost rings from pega to pegc	} 1
Attempting to solve the problem of moving 2 uppermost rings from pega to pegb	} 2
PRIMITIVE move exposed ring from pega to pegc	} 3
PRIMITIVE move exposed ring from pega to pegb	} 4
PRIMITIVE move exposed ring from pegc to pegb	} 5
PRIMITIVE move exposed ring from pega to pegc	} 6
Attempting to solve the problem of moving 2 uppermost rings from pegb to pegc	} 7
PRIMITIVE move exposed ring from pegb to pega	} 8
PRIMITIVE move exposed ring from pegb to pegc	} 9
PRIMITIVE move exposed ring from pega to pegc	} 10

Output chunk 1 is the output from the first call of solve_it, this problem requires decomposition by the problem reduction operator p_reduction. The first sub-problem is stated in output chunk 2. This recursive program decomposes the problem in a depth-first manner – that is, the first sub-problem will be completely solved before the second sub-problem is tackled. So the next job is to decompose the problem described in chunk 2. This requires a further application of our problem reduction operator. The first sub-problem of this further problem reduction is a primitive one (this is shown in output chunk 3). At this stage in the problem reduction, the second and third sub-problems are also primitive problems (shown in chunks 4 and 5). Having completed the analysis of this second call of the problem reduction operator we move up one level in the recursion and attend to the second sub-problem of the original problem decomposition. This also turns out to be a primitive problem – output chunk 6. However, the third sub-problem at this level of problem reduction requires another application of the reduction operator – output chunk 7. This is a two-ring problem and the stages represented in output chunks 8, 9 and 10 are analogous to those in 3, 4 and 5. These stages 1–10 represent a complete set of decomposed problems for the original problem description. You can see that a complete solution to the original problem is specified by the set comprising solutions to all of the primitive problems.

For this problem we have used an AND tree – that is, our problem reduction operator specified that a set of operations *all* had to be performed. However, as we stated earlier in this chapter, some problems require the search of AND/OR trees. This requires the combination of the problem reduction techniques outlined here, with search techniques such as those described in Chapter 7. In these more complex situations we need a way of searching **problem reduction spaces** themselves (rather than just state spaces as previously). To tackle full AND/OR trees we would need a general algorithm for searching them. Rather than spend the rest of this chapter presenting a POP-11 program to do this we refer the reader to Barr and Feigenbaum (1981). They provide a general algorithm in English, you might like to implement it in POP-11 for yourself.

We now turn to a rather different way of conducting goal directed behaviour.

9.2 The General Problem Solver

The work on GPS (the General Problem Solver) was begun in the late 50s by Newell, Shaw and Simon. Its most detailed presentation is to be found in Ernst and Newell (1969). Originally it was thought that research on GPS would provide both:

1. a problem solving mechanism for computers, and
2. a model of how humans solve problems.

However, over the years research on GPS has concerned itself with the first issue rather than the second.

GPS is so named because it attempts to separate out a problem solving mechanism from particular knowledge of the problem domain. The domain dependent knowledge comes in the form of objects and operators. A task in GPS consists of transforming an initial object into a desired object. At this point we can conceive of objects and operators as similar to the objects and operators of state space representations. What makes

GPS different from either the state space or problem reduction representations is the way it decides what to do when faced with the problem of transforming objects. It adopts a process known as Means-Ends Analysis (MEA). To help you understand MEA we will describe a possible application in a simple 'micro-world' of objects and operators.

Consider the following problem – we want to serve up some cake for tea. We go to the kitchen; if the cake is there we serve it up; if not we have three options. We can either make it ourselves, ring up and order one, or else go out and buy one.

If we decide to make one then we will need various ingredients; if we don't have any of them we will need to go and shop. To go shopping we would need some money. If we don't have any money then we will need to go to the bank. If we want to go to the bank we will have to work out a way of getting there.

This type of problem solving has a familiar look to it. How can we begin to formalize it so that we can construct a program to go through this type of behaviour? Using concepts from the GPS we can develop various operators and objects in this domain. In fact to characterize the operators we will use a formalism known as 'STRIPS'. STRIPS was originally developed by Fikes and Nilsson (1971) as a problem solving program. Each problem for STRIPS is a goal, each goal was originally meant to be achieved by a robot operating in a simple world of doors and boxes. The solution to a complex goal is a sequence of operators called a plan. The actual execution of the plan was carried out by a separate program distinct from STRIPS. So STRIPS was a problem solving system which implemented a 'planning system'. Since the first system, STRIPS-like formalisms have been widely used in a variety of AI contexts involving problem solving and planning.

The elements that make up the starting state in our 'cake' domain are given in Table 9.1 along with the goal state or final object. Notice that the representation used here is one that places a relationship first and then object(s) that enter into that relationship. We have met this 'predicate based' type of representation in Chapter 8. You will have noticed that some objects are not explicitly represented – thus the **have** relation or **in** relation is something that strictly holds between two objects, in this case the implied object is always the same – the person making the cake. There are a couple of further things to notice about this representation. When describing the initial state we assume the absence of a fact is equivalent to it not being true in the world. When specifying the facts that have to be true in the goal state we do not need exhaustively to describe the world – only those parts we are interested in. Therefore the goal state is not a representation of a complete world state.

Now to a representation of the operators. A number of STRIPS operators appear in Table 9.2. Each operator has a name, a set of preconditions, and a set of effects. The preconditions are things that have to be

Table 9.1 Starting state and goal state of the 'cake' domain.

'Relevant' start	'Relevant' goal
have[eggs]	have[cake]
have[flour]	in[kitchen]
have[money]	
have[car]	
in[kitchen]	

true in the world for the effects to occur. Effects are what happens if the preconditions are true and the operator is applied. Effects may be such as to make some things true in the world and others false. If we look at the operator **go_bank** we see that it has the effects of making it true that

one is in the bank – in[bank]

and not true that

one is somewhere else – in[elsewhere]

Table 9.2 Preconditions and effects of STRIPS operators.

Operator	Preconditions	Effects	
		Adds	Deletes
buy_cake	in[store], have[money]	have[cake]	have[money]
make_cake	have[eggs], have[flour] have[milk], have[sugar] in[kitchen]	have[cake]	have[eggs], have[milk], have[flour], have[sugar]
order_cake	in[kitchen], have[phone]	have[cake]	have[money]
buy_eggs	in[store], have[money]	have[eggs]	have[money]
buy_flour	in[store], have[money]	have[flour]	have[money]
go_bank	have[car]	in[bank]	in[elsewhere]
go_store	have[car]	in[store]	in[elsewhere]
go_kitchen	have[car]	in[kitchen]	in[elsewhere]
get_money	in[bank]	have[money]	

By representing our 'micro-world' in terms of these objects and operators we are representing it in a very minimal way. We only represent those objects and actions that are 'relevant' to the type of problem being tackled. It is of no relevance to the problem solving in this example that the telephone is a particular colour, or the car is of a certain make. Our operators only detail certain effects on the world. So the operator **go_store** ignores the fact that going somewhere in a car would use up fuel. The issue of what to include in such a problem and which operator descriptions are needed is one which you must decide upon for yourself. There is clearly a pay-off between how well your representation describes the world, and how much irrelevant detail is included in your description.

It is the application of MEA which determines the way various operators interact to achieve a goal. We shall now describe this mechanism. The driving force behind MEA is the detection of a difference between the current state of the world and the desired goal state. When a difference is detected the next job is to find an operator that will reduce the difference. This process continues recursively until the desired state of the world has been achieved. We shall see what this means in terms of our domain shortly.

An early method of implementing MEA was to use **goal stacks**. STRIPS operators fit into this method very naturally. This concept of a stack is the same as that employed in the POP-11 stack – the difference is in the things which we choose to store in these stacks. A goal stack is a single stack containing both goals (detected differences) and operators whose effects appear able to satisfy or solve these goals (reduce differences).

To see how all these components would go together in a problem solving system let's talk through the state of a goal stack in trying to solve the problem of getting a cake with the objects and operators supplied.

Using our goal stack we enter our initial problem description as a complex goal each component of which has to be jointly true in the world for the problem to be solved. At each stage in our use of the goal stack we work on the top element of the stack.

Our task after entering the problem description on the goal stack is to extract differences – differences are parts of the problem description that are not yet true in the world. Any differences that are found are entered as new goals onto the top of our goal stack. In our particular example a difference would be detected between the goal description and the world state – we do not have a cake! Difference extraction is the first phase of MEA.

At this stage our goal stack would consist of two elements, at the bottom of the stack the initial problem description (defined as the eventual goal), at the top of the stack the most recently extracted difference. Our current stack is represented below:

have[cake]
goal- have[cake] in[kitchen]

We shall be assuming that differences are extracted from left to right in complex goals and placed on the stack in the order in which they are extracted.

The next stage in MEA is to attempt to reduce any differences that have been detected. In our example we must attempt to find an operator, one of whose effects is to make it true that we have a cake.

Any program we write must at this stage be able to look at the operator table and select the operators that are applicable. With the operators as defined in Table 9.2 there are in fact three which have as their effects **have[cake]**.

At this point we are presented with a choice of which operator to use. Our program will not know ahead of time which operator is more likely to be successful, our only requirement will be that if one operator should not turn out to be successful any alternatives will be tried in a systematic way.

A number of things happen once a reducing operator has been found for a difference. The difference is removed from the top of the stack. It is then replaced by two elements: the 'reducing operator', and another complex goal which represents the preconditions of the 'reducing operator'. In this case suppose the first operator found in the operator table is **buy_cake**. Our stack is now:

> **goal- in[store] have[money]**
> **operator- buy_cake**
> **goal- have[cake] in[kitchen]**

As we have said, in order to apply the operator **buy[cake]** its preconditions, represented by the complex goal at the top of the stack, must be true. We must now go back to our cycle of extracting differences, establishing them as new goals and attempting to reduce any differences subsequently detected.

If we again extract differences on our goal stack we obtain:

> **in[store]**
> **goal- in[store] have[money]**
> **operator- buy_cake**
> **goal- have[cake] in[kitchen]**

You might be wondering why we keep the complex goals on the stack and do not simply replace them with sets of extracted differences. We will see later that we need to have a record of these goals in order to check that subsequent operations do not undo previously achieved goals. The ability to put right the undesired side-effects which may result as a consequence of achieving some goal is a crucial feature of effective problem solving.

An operator is now needed to reduce the new difference **in[store]**. One exists, **go_store**, the effects of which are to make it true that one is in the store and false that one is anywhere else. This operator together with its preconditions is added to the stack:

goal- have[car]
operator- go_store
goal- in[store] have[money]
operator- buy_cake
goal- have[cake] in[kitchen]

At this point the precondition for the operator **go_store** is fulfilled. We do not detect any differences between this goal and the state of our world. We can therefore apply the operator **go_store** and pop off the top two elements of the stack making sure we change the world in accordance with the effects of the operator. (We need a representation of the world in which we can represent the effects of operators.) Our goal stack is now:

goal- in[store] have[money]
operator- buy_cake
goal- have[cake] in[kitchen]

and the new world state is:

have[eggs] have[flour] have[car]
have[money] in[store]

Once again a complex goal is on top of the goal stack – one which previously had an unfulfilled precondition. The complex goal has no components which are not true in the world – and so once again we can apply the appropriate operator and pop off the top two elements from the stack making any changes to the world state. So we now have

goal stack:
    goal- have[cake] in[kitchen]

world state:
    have[eggs] have[flour] have[car]
    have[cake] in[store]

We are now back with our original complex goal. And we now see why it is important to record complex goals and always check that their preconditions are fulfilled whenever they are encountered. For on rechecking for differences we find that we have one – we are in the store not the kitchen! This is, of course, a consequence of an operator we have applied – **go_store** having an effect which is to delete a required and previously satisfied state. Such a difference can be reduced using the operator **go_kitchen**. The resulting stack using **go_kitchen** would be:

goal- have[car]
operator go_kitchen
goal- have[cake] in[kitchen]

No differences are now to be detected – the top two elements are removed and the relevant changes made. We now have

goal stack:
   goal- have[cake] in[kitchen]

world state:
   have[eggs] have[flour] have[car]
   have[cake] in[kitchen]

A final check is made to see that the preconditions of our original goal are satisfied. They are satisfied and the original problem description has been solved – we can pop it off the stack. We have solved our problem by applying the operators:

   go_store
   buy_cake
   go_kitchen

An important point to appreciate is that if we had selected our operators in a different order then different behaviour would have resulted. Suppose that **order_cake** had first been selected, and the alternatives were **buy_cake** and **make_cake** respectively.

A precondition of **order_cake** is **have[phone]**. Attempting to reduce the difference **have[phone]**, no operator would be found whose effects result in our having a phone. In this case we would have to back up and try an alternative way of solving the difference for which **order_cake** was originally called – this could be done by choosing one of the alternative operators **buy_cake** or **make_cake**.

A more complex back up would result if we changed our operator table so that we had no operator to get money and changed our world state so that we had no money. Suppose the order of extraction of the operators remains as in Table 9.2 top to bottom. MEA implemented using a single goal stack would produce the following behaviour. To solve **have[cake]** the operator **buy_cake** is called. Two differences are now observed – **in[store]** and **have[money]**. Because of the order of extraction the difference **in[store]** will be tackled first. There is an operator to reduce this difference, **go_store**; it will be applied, and its effects will change the world state – adding the fact **in[store]** and deleting the fact of being any-where else. We then have to try to reduce the difference **have[money]**, but there is no operator to do this. We have to back up to the last time an alternative operator was encountered in the problem solving. In this example this is when we tried to reduce the difference **have[cake]**. We will therefore have to undo any changes made to the world by operators after this point. We can see how important the process of backing up and remaking decisions is in this type of problem solving. But we also need to be able to undo any changes that have occurred beyond our point of backtrack.

We will now write a POP-11 program to do part of the MEA described above.

9.3 Writing GPS in POP-11

In the last section we developed a well specified characterization of the top level behaviour of the MEA process. We can use lists to represent our operators and our world state. The format we have used is shown below for part of the operator table and the complete world state. It makes it much easier to read large list structures if they are written as shown. The indentation displays the internal structure of the various lists.

The operator table is a list, each element of which is an operator definition. We have only shown one such operator, buy_cake. Each individual operator definition is simply a list of four lists. The first element of each of these four lists indicates what part of the structure of the operator we are representing – the remainder represents the content of that part of the operator structure. The first of the four embedded lists contains information about the name of the operator, the second indicates the preconditions for the operator, the third details the additions to make if the operator applies, and the fourth describes the deletions to make if the operator applies.

```
vars ops;
    [
        [
            [operator buy_cake]
            [preconditions [have [money]] [in [store]]]
            [additions [have [cake]]]
            [deletions [have [money]]]
        ]
            <+ OTHER OPERATORS>
    ] -> ops;
```

We can store the world state in the database as a list of lists each of which represents a true fact in the micro-world. We will do this inside a procedure, so that we can re-set the world to its initial state simply by calling the procedure:

```
define set_world();
[
    [have [eggs]]
    [have [flour]]
    [have [milk]]
    [have [money]]
    [have [car]]
    [in [kitchen]]
] -> database
enddefine;
```

In writing this 'partial' GPS program we are going to need a number of global variables to store various things in. We need a variable to represent the goal stack, a variable in which we will keep a record of the operators we successfully apply and a variable which is <false> unless the program cannot find a solution with the facts and operators provided.

```
vars goal_stack op_applied stuck;
[
    [goal [have [cake]] [in [kitchen]]]
] -> goal_stack;

[ ] -> op_applied;

false -> stuck;
```

Let us now consider the procedure which controls the way we use our goal stack. This procedure will include calls to other procedures which we have not yet defined. This way of building programs – defining the most general procedures first and then going on to define the 'nuts and bolts' procedures – is called **top down programming**. The alternative, building up from the nuts and bolts to the general, is called **bottom up programming**. We will build this program in a top down way so that you can always see why we are defining each procedure. Here is a definition of the topmost program control:

```
define control();
until goal_stack=[] or stuck
do  show_gstack();
    if goal_stack matches [[goal ==] ==]
    then extract_diff()
    else reduce_diff()
    endif
enduntil
enddefine;
```

This procedure establishes a loop which terminates if either the goal stack is empty or the global variable stuck has the value <true>. Each iteration through the loop contains a conditional test. The test finds out what is on top of the goal stack (i.e. at the front of the list goal_stack). If the top of the goal stack is a list whose first element is "goal" then the procedure responsible for extracting any differences is called. If we are not attempting to extract a difference then we must be attempting to reduce one. Hence the else condition in the conditional is the call of a procedure reduce_diff which attempts to reduce any differences that are found. Notice the presence of a call to a procedure show_gstack within control. This is a simple procedure that allows us to inspect the state of the goal stack on each iteration through the loop which control establishes – this procedure may be defined thus:

```
define show_gstack();
    ppr([goal stack is]); nl(1);
    goal_stack ==>
    nl(2)
enddefine;
```

Let us now look at a definition of a procedure to extract differences between the top of the goal stack and the state of the world.

```
1  define extract_diff();
2  vars comp_set rest_gstack;
3  ppr([attempting to extract differences]); nl(1);
4  goal_stack --> [[goal ??comp_set] ??rest_gstack];
5  until comp_set = []
6  do  if not(present(hd(comp_set)))
7        then [^(hd(comp_set)) ^^goal_stack] -> goal_stack
8        endif;
9        tl(comp_set) -> comp_set
10 enduntil;
11 if hd(goal_stack) matches [ goal ==]
12 then if rest_gstack = []
13      then [] -> goal_stack;
14            ppr([solved it using operators]); nl(1);
15            op_applied ==>
16      else rest_gstack -> goal_stack;
17            make_changes()
18      endif
19 endif
20 enddefine;
```

We know that a complex goal will match the pattern in line 4 of this procedure. Using the matcharrow the set of goals which make up the complex goal are stored in the local variable comp_set, and the rest of the goal stack is assigned to the local variable rest_gstack. The procedure then checks through the list comp_set comparing each element to the database. If an element of comp_set is not present then part of a complex goal is not true in the world – we have detected a difference and it is added as a separate goal to the top of the goal stack. This process of difference extraction continues until we have looked at all the elements in comp_set. The procedure extract_diff performs some other functions. At line 11 the goal stack is matched to see if the top element is a complex goal. This will only be true if no differences have been extracted by the previous part of the procedure. On line 12 it checks whether the complex goal at the top of the stack is the original problem description. This will be the case if the rest of the goal stack is empty. If this conditional test at line 12 returns <true> then we have actually solved the problem. If the conditional returns <false> then the complex conditions for an operator must have been satisfied and we pop the complex goal from off the stack and the procedure make_changes is called to apply the effects of the operator for which the preconditions have just been seen to be satisfied. Here is a definition of make_changes:

```
define make_changes();
vars name adds dels;
ppr([need to make changes]); nl(1);
hd(goal_stack) --> [operator ?name];
ops --> [== [[= ^name] = [= ??adds] [= ??dels]] ==];
until dels=[]
do   remove(hd(dels));
     tl(dels) -> dels
enduntil;
until adds=[]
do   add(hd(adds));
     tl(adds)->adds
enduntil;
tl(goal_stack) -> goal_stack;
ppr([world after success of ^name]); nl(1);
database==>
[^^op_applied ^name] -> op_applied
enddefine;
```

When make_changes is called we are guaranteed that an operator will be on top of the goal stack. In order to make the changes we first determine from the operator table what the effects of the operator at the top of the stack are. This is done in two matching operations: matching first against the goal stack to get the name of the operator, and secondly matching against the operator table to get the operator's adds and deletes. Any deletions that are required are picked up in a local variable list called dels and any additions in a local list adds. The dels list is iterated through until it is empty and any elements in it are removed from the world stored in the database – notice we can use the built-in database facility to do this. A similar iteration is made on the adds list except, of course, the elements are added to the world state. Finally the operator is removed from the top of the goal stack and its name is added to the global list op_applied which contains a list of operators successfully applied.

Having considered the extraction of differences we will now turn to the business of difference reduction. As we have mentioned the top level procedure control works by assuming that if it is not extracting differences then it must be reducing differences. If the top element of the goal stack is a complex goal the program will attempt to extract differences – otherwise it must be attempting to reduce differences. The procedure reduce_diff can be defined as follows:

```
define reduce_diff();
vars app_ops name precons temp;
[] -> app_ops;
ppr([trying to reduce differences]); nl(1);
ops -> temp;
until temp = []
do  if hd(temp) matches
          [[= ?name] [= ??precons] [== ^(hd(goal_stack)) ==] =]
      then [^^app_ops [^name ^precons]] -> app_ops
      endif;
      tl(temp) -> temp
enduntil;
if app_ops = []
then ppr([no operator to reduce difference]); nl(1);
     ppr([need to backup]); nl(2);
     true -> stuck
else pick_op(app_ops)
endif
enddefine;
```

The procedure reduce_diff iterates through the operator table finding any
operator whose add list has an element which matches the current difference, i.e. the top of the current goal stack. Each time one is detected
its name together with its preconditions are stored in the local variable
app_ops. After this process has ended we check the state of app_ops, it may
be that no operator has been found to reduce the current difference – if
this is the case our program will signal that back up has to occur. If
app_ops is not empty we need to select an operator, this is done through
the procedure pick_op which takes as its argument the list of operators
contained in app_ops.

```
define pick_op(list);
vars n p r;
list --> [ [?n ?p] ??r];
ppr([selected operator ^n to reduce ^(hd(goal_stack))]); nl(1);
if length(list) > 1
then
    ppr([alternative operators exist to reduce ^(hd(goal_stack))]);
    nl(1)
endif;
[[goal ^^p] [operator ^n] ^^(tl(goal_stack))] -> goal_stack
enddefine;
```

The pick_op procedure is straightforward: it extracts the name and preconditions of the first operator in the list of applicable operators and places
two new elements on the goal stack. At the top of the stack is a complex

goal consisting of the preconditions of the operator, and below it is an element representing the name of the operator. Notice these elements are appended to the tail of the goal stack – thus the operator replaces the difference. The procedure then checks to see if the remainder of the operator list contains any other operators; if it does then a message is printed to indicate that alternative operator choices could have been made.

9.4 A run of the program

Suppose we now run our program on the operators as given and ordered in Table 9.2. A call of `control` on such an operator table with the world state as shown on page 136 provides the following output:

```
: control();

goal stack is
** [[goal [have [cake]] [in [kitchen]]]]

attempting to extract differences
goal stack is
** [[have [cake]]
    [goal [have [cake]] [in [kitchen]]]]
```

At this point we can see that the program has extracted the first difference, and it becomes the new top element of the stack. As we see in the subsequent output the program tries to reduce this difference.

```
trying to reduce differences
selected operator buy_cake to reduce have cake
alternative operators exist to reduce have cake
goal stack is
** [[goal [have [money]] [in [store]]]
    [operator buy_cake]
    [goal [have [cake]] [in [kitchen]]]]
```

In the previous section of output an operator was found to reduce the difference [have [cake]]; notice, however, that other operators were also detected which could reduce this difference. The new operator has its preconditions added to the stack and the process of difference extraction begins again.

```
attempting to extract differences
goal stack is
** [[in [store]]
    [goal [have [money]] [in [store]]]
    [operator buy_cake]
    [goal [have [cake]] [in [kitchen]]]]
```

```
trying to reduce differences
selected operator go_store to reduce in store
goal stack is
** [[goal [have [car]]]
    [operator go_store]
    [goal [have [money]] [in [store]]]
    [operator buy_cake]
    [goal [have [cake]] [in [kitchen]]]]
```

The operator buy_cake has an unfulfilled precondition, [in [store]], we
see above that an operator has been found to reduce the difference and in
turn its preconditions have been added to the stack. All the preconditions
of this operator go_store are true – it is applied and the world state is
changed giving the output shown below:

```
attempting to extract differences
need to make changes
world after success of go_store
** [[in [store]]
    [have [eggs]]
    [have [flour]]
    [have [milk]]
    [have [money]]
    [have [car]]]

goal stack is
** [[goal [have [money]] [in [store]]]
    [operator buy_cake]
    [goal [have [cake]] [in [kitchen]]]]
```

Once go_store has succeeded then the original difference contained in the
preconditions of buy_cake has been reduced. The program therefore
applies the operator and changes the world state.

```
attempting to extract differences
need to make changes
world after success of buy_cake
** [[have [cake]]
    [in [store]]
    [have [eggs]]
    [have [flour]]
    [have [milk]]
    [have [car]]]

goal stack is
** [[goal [have [cake]] [in [kitchen]]]]
```

Notice that the goal stack now only contains the original problem
description – but a new difference can be detected as we see below. The

difference has arisen because an operator used to reduce a previous difference, namely go_store, deleted a precondition of the original problem description, i.e. the fact [in [kitchen]]. The final part of the output detects this difference and reduces it producing a complete set of operators to solve the original problem.

```
attempting to extract differences
goal stack is
** [[in [kitchen]]
   [goal [have [cake]] [in [kitchen]]]]

trying to reduce differences
selected operator go_kitchen to reduce in kitchen
goal stack is
** [[goal [have [car]] ]
   [operator go_kitchen]
   [goal [have [cake]] [in [kitchen]]]]

attempting to extract differences
need to make changes
world after success of go_kitchen
** [[in [kitchen]]
   [have [cake]]
   [have [eggs]]
   [have [flour]]
   [have [milk]]
   [have [car]]]

goal stack is
** [[goal [have [cake]] [in [kitchen]]]]

attempting to extract differences
solved it using operators
** [go_store buy_cake go_kitchen]
```

This program run is, in fact, a replica of the talk-through we performed when we introduced GPS. We made the point in the talk-through that different orderings of operators can produce different behaviour. We will now look at what happens when we work in the context described on page 140, where the operator order_cake is selected first – this fails ultimately because we have no operator to achieve one of its preconditions [have [phone]]. At this point our program stops because we have not given it a backtrack facility. What should happen is that the program should backtrack to the last point where alternative operators existed to reduce a difference and should pursue the alternative operator to see if a solution path can be found. This process should be a general one – it should be able to apply to any alternatives chosen.

The output below indicates that the program has noted that alternative operators exist for reducing some differences – what is missing is the ability to restore various variables to the values they had when the alternative was encountered and to proceed from there. We leave this additional feature as a programming problem you might like to tackle.

```
: control();

goal stack is
** [[goal [have [cake]] [in [kitchen]]]]

attempting to extract differences
goal stack is
** [[have [cake]]
    [goal [have [cake]] [in [kitchen]]]]

trying to reduce differences
selected operator order_cake to reduce have cake
alternative operators exist to reduce have cake
goal stack is
** [[goal [in [kitchen]] [have [phone]]]
    [operator order_cake]
    [goal [have [cake]] [in [kitchen]]]]

attempting to extract differences
goal stack is
** [[have [phone]]
    [goal [in [kitchen]] [have [phone]]]
    [operator order_cake]
    [goal [have [cake]] [in [kitchen]]]]

trying to reduce differences
no operator to reduce difference
need to backup
```

Many issues are raised by our discussion of GPS. We have a problem solving device that can work over any domain which we can represent using operator tables and objects. The problem solving is independent of the domain. To see this you might like to run this program on a completely different set of operators and objects.

Another issue is the familiar one of search strategy. We can see how sensitive GPS is to the order in which alternative operators are tried. A program such as this may go a long way down what is ultimately a blind alley, only to have to back up. This has led AI researchers to develop programs which attempt to make more intelligent decisions about which operators to apply first. We have also met the issue of interactions between sub-goals – some operators undo solutions required by other operators.

A final point to note: we might wonder how we can introduce 'generalized operators' into our program. Instead of having many operators of the form:

buy_eggs	**in[store], have[money]**	**have[eggs]**	**have[money]**
buy_flour	**in[store], have[money]**	**have[flour]**	**have[money]**

why not have a generalization of the form:

buy_x	**in[store], have[money]**	**have[x]**	**have[money]**

We then fill in the variable slots as appropriate in working through the solution. Such a generalization would have required some clever programming so as to be able to assign and deassign the variables in the rules as the program worked through the problem space. As an exercise you might think about the problems involved in implementing such a facility.

This chapter has served as a very elementary introduction to planning. We have built two simple planning systems in order to demonstrate some classic issues in this area. However, planning is very much a 'live' topic in AI, and there is currently a great deal of effort being put in to developing increasingly intelligent planning systems. In Chapter 11 we point to a couple of recent projects which the reader interested in technical issues may want to follow up. However, a more general overview of the area can be found in Charniak and McDermott (1985; Chapter 9). On our part, we hope that we have successfully introduced the reader to some of the more important aspects of the topic, and shown how POP-11 can be used to implement the type of program used in planning. In the next chapter we consider another central topic in AI – natural language processing.

Chapter 10 Natural Language Processing

10.1 Introduction

Language is one of humankind's most prized capabilities, and yet it is one we take very much for granted. As with many of our cognitive abilities, we are too close to the phenomenon to appreciate its complexity. As was stated in the first chapter, artificial intelligence, whatever else it does, demonstrates the complexity of what, to us, is routine behaviour.

Historically, the problem of getting machines to understand and generate language was one of the first areas of AI research. Then as now one of the biggest investors in computer research was the Military. It has always had a close involvement with computers, psychology and AI. During the Second World War some of the earliest computer science was directed towards the problem of encrypting and deciphering enemy intelligence.

The increased sophistication of electronic surveillance techniques meant that by the late 50s and early 60s the US military were being overwhelmed by the sheer amount of intelligence coming in. You will not be surprised to learn that much of this material was in the Russian language. There were not enough skilled translators to deal with this mountain of material. The idea of computers doing the job quickly and cheaply was therefore very attractive. Machine translation was the goal, and many millions of dollars were spent towards this end.

There was an early realization that the only way to solve the problem of machine translation required that we understand the rules and structure that lie behind language. This was an ambitious program and early attempts to get 'language' out of computers did not apply a thorough and principled approach, they 'cheated'.

Cheat programs did not have 'knowledge' of language, language structure, or the domain of discourse. They relied on finding predefined patterns and issuing limited responses to these patterns. Nevertheless natural language interfaces (NLIs) that use pattern matching sometimes have the appearance of linguistic competence – beware of these imitations!

To talk in any serious way about natural language processing requires that we provide the system with knowledge about the system of language itself. What does this mean? How do we represent this information computationally?

10.2 Levels of organization in language

Language is rule-governed. This fundamental fact is reaffirmed whenever we look at the rules violated in examples such as (1)–(6).

1. Gblick hgn tched.
2. The boy hit girl the head the on.
3. The boy jump the fence.
4. The boys jumps the fence.
5. Steaks eat stones.
6. Nigel asks of Mike 'Can you pass the salt'. Mike looks up, answers 'Yes', but carries on eating.

In (1) the rules that are being broken are those rules in English which determine which combinations of sounds constitute legal sequences. In English we do not have the sorts of consonant sequences shown in (1). Nonsense words such as 'blik' and 'strot' etc. may be nonsense but they do not violate sound sequence rules. English also requires that words occur in a certain order when building up sentences: (2) does not obey these rules. In (3) and (4) the relation of 'agreement' is being broken. In English, subject and verb must agree according to the following rules:

> If the subject of a sentence is a singular noun then the verb is in the 3rd person singular.

> If the subject of a sentence is a plural noun then the verb is unmarked.

In (5) we have a correct combination of grammatical categories but the resulting sentence is nonsense; we have violated the rules of semantics. Finally, in (6) we have yet another type of rule breaking; we would say that the respondent is being uncooperative by not going beyond the literal meaning of what was said and complying with the request that lies behind Nigel's utterance.

The rules that are being broken operate at distinct levels. We distinguish these levels in the following way:

> The phonological level – the sound system of a language;
>
> The syntactic level   – the grammar of a language;
>
> The semantic level   – the rules of meaning of language;
>
> The pragmatic level   – non-linguistic knowledge that allows
>   us to interpret language.

These levels of language organization have served as separate areas of linguistic and psychological study. All of these levels interact to produce the total system we refer to as language.

AI has devoted considerable attention to one particular area of language – namely, syntax. There are good reasons for this:

1. Syntax has an obvious formal structure;
2. It does not require special hardware to start research – study of computational phonology might require synthesizers, etc.;
3. Detailed theories of syntactic structure appeared at the time computational linguistics first got started.

Phrase Structure Grammars were amongst the first theories of syntactic structure to be utilized by AI researchers.

10.3 Phrase Structure Grammars – the syntactic level

A Phrase Structure Grammar can best be illustrated by considering our intuitions about a sentence such as (7).

7. The students run away.

There seem to be two main components to this sentence: 'the students' and 'run away'. These in turn are two-element sub-structures. We can propose a structure for (7) such as shown in Figure 10.1.

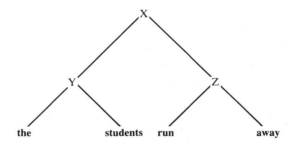

Figure 10.1 The syntactic approach.

The work of modern linguists, in particular that of Noam Chomsky, has been concerned to provide sets of such decompositions for a wide range of sentences. Once you have rules of decomposition you can use them 'backwards' as rules of sentence generation. We refer to the process of decomposition as **sentence parsing**; the opposite process is known simply as **sentence generation**.

Phrase Structure Grammars are technically 'rewrite systems'. We have already met rules very much like grammar rules in those used for production systems. Both sets of rules have symbols on their left hand sides which can be expanded to give the constituents represented on their right hand sides. Using a few common grammatical conventions to name grammatical constituents we can frame a set of rules such as those shown in Figure 10.2.

(i)   Sentence ⟶ Noun Phrase + Verb Phrase

(ii) Verb Phrase ⟶ Verb + Adverb

(iii) Noun Phrase ⟶ Determiner + Noun

Figure 10.2 A set of grammar rules.

Suppose we apply the rules in sequence, i.e. (i), (ii) and (iii). We can trace this sequence of applications in terms of the growth of the structures shown in Figure 10.3.

Together with these rewrite rules a Phrase Structure Grammar also provides a 'lexicon' – this is a way of realizing certain 'terminal' grammatical categories as words in a language. A small lexicon is given below – we see for example that the grammatical class 'verb' contains words such as 'run', 'stop', 'work', etc. If we now 'plug' instances of these 'terminal categories' into the final structure shown in Figure 10.3 we could generate the sentence given in (7).

Noun   = {students, girls, boys, computers,...}
Verb   = {run, stop, work,...}
Determiner = {the, some,...}
Adverb   = {away, slowly,...}

What we have provided in a Phrase Structure Grammar is a model of the syntactic structure of a fragment of English. Let's start to think about how this simple account of sentence structure could be realized as a program – as a computational model.

10.4 Sentence generation

The first program we will look at generates sentences; it uses the very simple grammar and lexicon we described in the previous section. The program makes use of a modified form of the production system developed in Chapter 8.

Remember that a production system consists of a set of productions, a context and an interpreter. The productions allow us to generate new symbols from those existing already in the context. Applying productions

Rule (i)

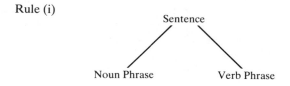

Rule (ii)

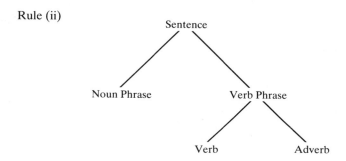

Rule (iii)

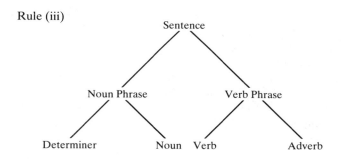

Figure 10.3 Applying the set of rules from Figure 10.2.

may mean that symbols remain unchanged, be modified, or be removed from the context. These symbols may represent many kinds of knowledge or information. In Chapter 8 they represented actions and instructions to do with preparing simple meals. Our production rules require an inter-preter, the interpreter applies our rules in a certain way. The one built in Chapter 8 simply went through the list of rules applying any that it could in order, from the beginning of the rule-set until it met a stopping condi-tion in a later rule.

In constructing a production system for sentence generation we must first consider how our knowledge of grammar translates into production rules. The translation is, in fact, very straightforward since grammar rules and production rules are both types of rewrite system. The database variable below contains a set of list elements each of which represents a grammar rule. Thus the first element of database is a two-element list: the first element is a list containing the LHS symbol; the second is a list containing the instruction to expand the LHS symbol into new constituents.

```
[
    [[Sentence]    [
                   [putin NounPhrase VerbPhrase for Sentence]
                   ]]

    [[VerbPhrase]  [
                   [putin Verb Adverb for VerbPhrase]
                   ]]

    [[NounPhrase]  [
                   [putin Determiner Noun for NounPhrase]
                   [Last]
                   ]]
] -> database;
```

Our system will use the grammar rules as productions to change the context. The context starts with an initial symbol, productions replace it with legal sub-parts. The processing continues until the context consists entirely of terminal symbols.

With one exception the single action in the production system is to replace material in the context with new material as determined by the application of various productions. The exception is the final rule which contains an additional item of information – indicating that it is the last rule in the database – this is used to provide a stopping condition for our production system interpreter.

Our context is set up as a global variable containing the starting symbol "Sentence".

```
vars context;
[Sentence] -> context;
```

Our interpreter is exactly the same as that given on page 124; it is reproduced below. The procedure interpreter examines each rule in turn and performs the action specified by the rule if the left hand side (LHS) of the rule is present in the context. This LHS condition is tested by the procedure lhs, the form of which is only slightly different from that given in Chapter 8.

```
define interpreter();
vars l r stopper;
false -> stopper;
until stopper
```

```
do  foreach [?l ?r]
    do  if lhs(l)
        then rhs(r)
        endif
    endforeach
enduntil
enddefine;

define lhs(cond);
vars item;
if context matches [== ^(hd(cond)) ==]
then true
else false
endif
enddefine;
```

The procedure lhs is simpler than that given on page 123, since in this case there is only one type of LHS. So we do not have to look for different types of LHS. The procedure looks to see if the symbol contained in the LHS of the rule is present in the context. If it is then it returns <true> otherwise it returns <false>.

The procedure rhs is exactly as we defined in Chapter 8. The procedure allows us to look at each part of the RHS of a rule and carry out the set of operations specified therein.

There are only two types of operation contained in the RHSs of our production rules. These are catered for in a new version of obeyact.

```
define rhs(acts);
until acts = []
do  obeyact(hd(acts));
    tl(acts) -> acts
enduntil
enddefine;

1  define obeyact(list);
2  vars x y lc rc;
3  if list matches [putin ??x for ?y]
4  then if context matches [??lc ^y ??rc]
5      then [^^lc ^^x ^^rc] -> context;
6           [expanding ^y to ^^x] =>
7           context =>
8      endif
9  elseif list = [Last]
10 then true -> stopper
11 endif
12 enddefine;
```

The procedure obeyact performs two types of operation depending on the type of RHS component found. The RHS of a rule can be an instruction to replace a symbol in the context with another symbol or symbols. This is achieved in lines 3 to 5 of obeyact; notice that the replacement is carried out in such a way that the new symbols replace the old symbol in the same position in context. The other type of operation is to test to see if we are dealing with the last rule in the database. If we are, then the global variable stopper has its value set to <true> – this will halt the process of rule interpretation.

An example of the program's normal output is given below.

```
: interpreter();
** [expanding Sentence to NounPhrase VerbPhrase]
** [NounPhrase VerbPhrase]
** [expanding VerbPhrase to Verb Adverb]
** [NounPhrase Verb Adverb]
** [expanding NounPhrase to Determiner Noun]
** [Determiner Noun Verb Adverb]
```

Finally we will replace our terminal grammatical categories with words of the appropriate type from a lexicon. The lexicon we can represent as a list structure. One way of doing this is shown in the content of the global variable lexicon. A procedure insert_words is also defined which iterates through the context taking each terminal and randomly selecting a word out of the lexicon which is of the terminal's grammatical type. Our procedure insert_words uses the built-in procedure oneof, which randomly selects an element from a list; insert_words substitutes the selected word for the terminal category.

```
vars lexicon;
[   [Noun [students girls boys computers]]
    [Determiner [the some]]
    [Verb [run stop work]]
    [Adverb [slowly away]]
] -> lexicon;

define insert_words();
vars n chosen_word words;
1 -> n;
until n > length(context)
do  if lexicon matches [== [^(context(n)) ?words] ==]
    then oneof(words) -> chosen_word;
         chosen_word -> context(n);
         n+1 -> n
    endif
enduntil;
context ==>
enddefine;
```

Output from our complete set of procedures is illustrated below.

```
:interpreter();
** [expanding Sentence to NounPhrase VerbPhrase]
** [NounPhrase VerbPhrase]
** [expanding VerbPhrase to Verb Adverb]
** [NounPhrase Verb Adverb]
** [expanding NounPhrase to Determiner Noun]
** [Determiner Noun Verb Adverb]
:insert_words();
** [the girls work away]
```

Suppose we wanted to extend the scope of our grammar – to add some new rules so as to generate a larger set of sentences. We will add the following additional rules that represent different ways of expanding a verb phrase.

Verb_Phrase → VerbI
Verb_Phrase → VerbI Adverb
Verb_Phrase → VerbT Noun_Phrase
Verb_Phrase → VerbT Noun_Phrase Adverb

In these rules we have distinguished two types of verb phrase – transitive and intransitive verb phrases. They contain two different categories of verb. Transitive verbs such as 'kiss' and 'love' require both a subject and an object, they allow us to construct sentences such as 'the students kiss the girls'. Intransitive verbs require only a subject, thus verbs such as 'run' and 'work' form sentences like 'the boys run' and so on. Notice that the category of adverb can occur in both types of verb phrase. In fact an adverbial constituent can be regarded as an *optional* constituent. In linguistic theory we often distinguish rules which introduce optional constituents from those that introduce *obligatory* ones. The rule for expanding a sentence introduces two obligatory elements, a noun phrase and a verb phrase. These obligatory constituents must be present for our little grammar to work at all. However, we shall not pursue the distinction between these two types of constituent any further.

How can we introduce these new rules into our sentence generation program? There is a problem with just extending our database by simply adding new elements corresponding to the new rules.

As it stands, our interpreter imposes an ordering on which rules stand a chance of being executed. The control of the interpreter is:

1. Start at the beginning of the rule-set.

2. If the rule is satisfied then apply it.

3. If the rule is the last rule then stop.

4. Consider the next rule in the rule-set, go to (2).

This means that the interpreter will always apply the first applicable rule for any constituent it finds in the context. A slight alteration to the way rules are represented would allow more varied behaviour. Our new rules are all expansions of the same grammatical constituent – a verb phrase. Suppose we represent the database as shown below. One element of database represents the fact that a verb phrase can expand in one of four ways.

```
[
    [[Sentence]     [[
                    [putin NounPhrase VerbPhrase for Sentence]
                    ]]]

    [[VerbPhrase]   [[
                    [putin VerbI for VerbPhrase]
                    [putin VerbI Adverb for VerbPhrase]
                    [putin VerbT NounPhrase for VerbPhrase]
                    [putin VerbT NounPhrase Adverb for VerbPhrase]
                    ]]]

    [[NounPhrase]   [
                    [
                    [putin Determiner Noun for NounPhrase]
                    ]
                    [Last]
                    ]]
] -> database;
```

We now make a small change to obeyact, we make the procedure select at random a member of its input. This means that, if there are alternatives, the interpreter need not necessarily always select the same expansion of a particular grammatical constituent.

```
define obeyact(list);
vars x y lc rc;
if oneof(list) matches [putin ??x for ?y]
then if context matches [??lc ^y ??rc]
    then [^^lc ^^x ^^rc] -> context;
        [expanding ^y to ^^x] =>
        context =>
    endif
elseif list = [Last]
then true -> stopper
endif
enddefine;
```

A sample run of the program might give us the behaviour shown below.

```
: interpreter();
** [expanding Sentence to NounPhrase VerbPhrase]
** [NounPhrase VerbPhrase]
** [expanding VerbPhrase to VerbI]
** [NounPhrase VerbI]
** [expanding NounPhrase to Determiner Noun]
** [Determiner Noun VerbI]
```

But it might also give us,

```
: interpreter();
** [expanding Sentence to NounPhrase VerbPhrase]
** [NounPhrase VerbPhrase]
** [expanding VerbPhrase to VerbT NounPhrase]
** [NounPhrase VerbT NounPhrase]
** [expanding NounPhrase to Determiner Noun]
** [Determiner Noun VerbT NounPhrase]
```

This has selected the rule for expanding a verb phrase as a transitive verb and a noun phrase. But notice that in the final line of output we still have an unexpanded category – the last noun phrase in the list. The problem here is that our interpreter is only making one pass through the rule-set. It only applies the rule to expand a noun phrase once – and it applies it to the first element in the relevant list that satisfies the specified pattern.

We need a way of making multiple passes through the production rules and finally stopping when no more rules are applicable. We need to modify our interpreter. How can this be done? One way of approaching the problem is to consider turning interpreter into a recursive procedure. Our stopping condition would be a situation in which we had passed through the entire rule-set without a single rule having been applied. This would indicate that no symbols were left in context that could be expanded. Until this stopping condition was encountered we would go through our rule-set expanding symbols; on reaching the end of the rule-set we would recursively call up the procedure interpreter. The definition of interpreter given below implements just such a control strategy.

```
1   define interpreter();
2   vars l r anyfired;
3   if it matches [[=] [= [Last]] ] and anyfired = false
4   then
5   else false -> anyfired;
6       [] -> it;
7       foreach [?l ?r]
8       do  if lhs(l)
9           then rhs(r);
10          true -> anyfired
11          endif
```

```
12        endforeach;
13        interpreter()
14 endif
15 enddefine;
```

Our stopping condition is embodied in line 3 of the definition. We are using two variables in this conditional. Firstly, the database variable it, this takes as its value the most recent database element used by the standard database procedures. In this case it is the most recent database element used by foreach. Secondly, we make a check on a local variable anyfired. The first part of the conditional in line 3 checks whether the last element used by foreach was the last rule in the database and the second part checks to see if the local variable anyfired has the value <false>. If both of these conditions are met then the procedure interpreter does not subsequently call itself. The variable anyfired will only have the value <false> if none of the rules in the database has fired this time through the rule-set. If any rules had fired then anyfired would have been assigned the value <true> (see lines 7–12). Moreover, the resulting symbol expansion might have produced a non-terminal symbol which could not get expanded this time through the rule-set because the relevant rule has already been encountered. It is to cover this eventuality that a recursive call must be made at line 13 of our definition.

With this type of interpreter we can now go on to make some more interesting extensions to our grammar. Let us extend and modify our grammar so that it now contains the rules shown below.

Sentence   → Noun_Phrase Verb_Phrase
Verb_Phrase   → VerbI
Verb_Phrase   → VerbI Adverb
Verb_Phrase   → VerbT Noun_Phrase
Verb_Phrase   → VerbT Noun_Phrase Adverb
Noun_Phrase   → Determiner Noun_Nucleus
Noun_Nucleus   → Adjective Noun_Nucleus
Noun_Nucleus   → Noun

Our new grammar has a very important feature. It now contains a recursive grammar rule: a noun nucleus can expand into an adjective and a noun nucleus. Language has this recursive property – the sentences below have been recursively extended and could in principle be expanded along similar lines indefinitely. Any viable model of linguistic processing must be able to cope with these recursive structures in language.

(a)   The man cried.

(a′) The old man cried.

(a″) The wise old man cried.

(a‴) The sad wise old man cried.

(b)   The boy put the toy in the box.

(b')   The boy put the toy in the box in the cupboard.

(b")   The boy put the toy in the box in the cupboard in the playroom.

Just as with our programming procedures we need rules in our grammar to halt indefinite expansion of recursive categories. This is the function of the rule:

Noun_Nucleus → Noun

This provides an alternative way of expanding the category noun nucleus which results in a non-recursively expandable item, in this case the terminal category noun.

With the appropriate extensions to database and lexicon we can implement this new grammar and get interesting sentence structures generated. We leave this as an exercise for the student. Of course, some of the results can start to look a bit tedious, repetitive and semantically queer if our oneof procedure keeps selecting a recursive grammar rule and certain words out of the lexicon.

Suppose we add another recursive grammar rule. This is a rule to conjoin two noun nuclei.

Noun_Nucleus → Noun_Nucleus Conjunction Noun_Nucleus

This rule provides a grammar able to generate sentences such as:

the young boys and girls admire the computers.

An interesting feature about this sentence emerges when we consider its possible generative history. There are in fact two syntactic structures that could underlie the sentence, corresponding to two different derivational histories and to two sets of grammar rule application.

This difference is highlighted if we consider the two ways in which the phrase 'the young boys and girls' can be understood. Are both the boys and girls young? Or are the boys young and the girls of some indeterminate age? Another way of conceiving of this difference is to ask whether the adjective modifies both of the nouns in the conjunct or just the first. We might argue that this syntactic difference is responsible for the ambiguity of meaning apparent in the final sentence. We are thus modelling one aspect of how sentences come to have the meanings they do.

Follow through for yourselves the structural differences which result from expanding the noun phrase using either the sequence of rules:

NounPhrase   → det NounNucleus
NounNucleus → Adjective NounNucleus
NounNucleus → NounNucleus Conjunction NounNucleus
NounNucleus → Noun
NounNucleus → Noun

or

> NounPhrase   → det NounNucleus
> NounNucleus → NounNucleus Conjunction NounNucleus
> NounNucleus → Adjective NounNucleus
> NounNucleus → Noun
> NounNucleus → Noun

As an exercise you should incorporate these rules into the program and generate for yourselves various syntactic structures.

10.5 Sentence parsing

Let us now consider the reverse process to sentence generation – that of sentence parsing. We will present a simple program to illustrate the basic idea of the process as well as introducing an important method used in computational linguistics – transition networks.

Consider the sentences below:

1. The boys kiss the girls.
2. The boys the kiss girls.

How are we to move from the surface set of words in (1) to some sort of decision about the well-formedness of the sentence? In the case of both (1) and (2) how are we to decide that (1) is grammatical and (2) ungrammatical?

As soon as we start to think about this problem we realize that there are two ways of tackling it. The two contrasting approaches are known as 'top down' and 'bottom up' processing. Let's suppose we have a very simple grammar and lexicon such as that shown below.

> S   → NP VP
> NP → det noun
> VP → verbt NP
>
> noun = {students, girls, boys, computers}
> verbt = {love, program, see}
> det   = {the, some}

Suppose we wish to decide if the following list of words is a grammatical sentence: 'the boys see the girls'. A top down approach works by setting up expectations that a sentence or 'S' constituent will be found in our list of words. It then uses the grammar rules to determine which rules are expansions for an 'S' category. In our grammar there is only one and it generates two new expectations: that we should find an 'NP' constituent followed by a 'VP' constituent. The grammar rules are being used as left to right rewrite rules. Starting with top level constituents the process of parsing progressively establishes expectations about what lower level constituents might be encountered. The top down approach illustrated in this section is also 'depth-first'; after the rule 'S → NP VP' is applied, the NP constituent is expanded first. The order in which rules would be applied and a parse conducted for our list of words is reflected in the progressive construction of **parse trees** shown in Figure 10.4

By contrast bottom up parsing requires that we apply a grammar rule backwards, that is we use the right hand side of the rule to determine what the left hand side which generated it could have been. Once again suppose we are given the sentence 'the boys see the girls'. The first stage in bottom up parsing is to determine the grammatical category of the first word encountered (lexical entries can be thought of as abbreviated rules of the sort 'det → the', 'det → some' etc.). Obviously 'the' is a 'det', having made this match we replace the part matched by the left hand side of the 'rule'. By consistently doing this we generate a complete parse. Again we can see the progressive nature of the bottom up parsing algorithm if we look at Figure 10.5.

This is all straightforward. However, things get more complex when we consider grammars which have a number of ways of expanding any given constituent. We might, for example, have a number of ways of expanding a noun phrase or verb phrase constituent. Lexical items might belong to more than one grammatical category, for example, the word 'can' may be a main verb, an auxiliary verb or a noun.

1. The students can fruit.
2. The students can take a holiday.
3. The students get the fruit from a can.

When faced with these multiple options strict top down and bottom up parsers have no alternative but to try the various possibilities until one is found that works in the context of the particular sentence being parsed. It should be obvious that this will require some form of backtracking facility to previous choice points.

For the rest of this chapter we will concentrate on building a top down parser using the concept of **transition networks**. Transition nets are usually introduced using a simple graphical notation. The concepts behind such nets are very simple, and provide a different way of describing a set of grammatical rules. First we will define a grammar which we want to encapsulate in our transition nets – we will initially describe it in a familiar set of rewrite rules.

Rule 1. s   → np vp
Rule 2. np → det noun
Rule 3. np → pname
Rule 4. vp → verbi
Rule 5. vp → verbt np

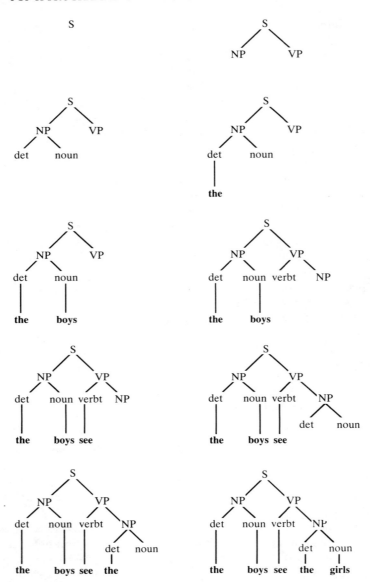

Figure 10.4 The progressive construction of 'parse trees' using the top down approach.

We will also assume a familiar and simple lexicon.

```
det    = {the, a}
noun   = {boy, girl, dog, computer}
pname  = {steve, ben, fiona, wendy}
```

verbi = {walks, sleeps, cries}
verbt = {loves, sees, admires}

Let us now convert our grammar into a transition net notation. The first rule of our grammar would be represented as network (i) in Figure 10.6.

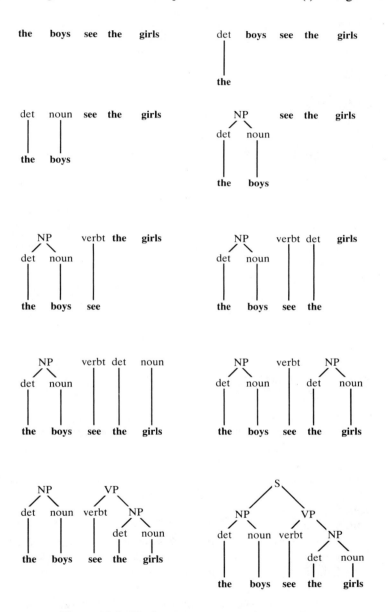

Figure 10.5 The bottom up approach to parsing.

Transition nets use the arc and node form of representation which we have met elsewhere in this book.

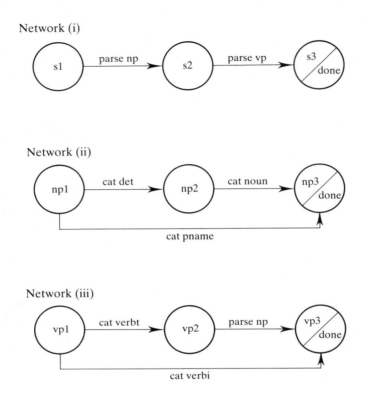

Network (i)

Network (ii)

Network (iii)

Figure 10.6 We can represent a grammar using the concept of transition networks.

The first node in a network contains the name of the constituent for which the rest of the net is a set of parsing instructions. In the case of network (i) this is node 's1' – the first node in a transition net for a sentence. To proceed to the next node, 's2', we must traverse the directed arc leaving 's1'. The arc can be understood as specifying an action to be performed. The action on this arc is 'parse np'. If this action can be performed we can pass to 's2'. There is now one arc from 's2' to 's3', this requires that we should 'parse vp'. If this action is performed successfully there are no arcs leaving 's3', in fact this node has a feature 'done' which indicates that if this node is reached the constituent 's' has been parsed.

How is the action 'parse np' interpreted? In transition nets this instruction requires that we find a network which in turn will tell us how to parse an 'np' constituent – find a network whose first node is 'np1'.

Networks (ii) and (iii) in Figure 10.6 are nets for noun phrases and verb phrases. Notice that some of the nodes in these nets have more than one arc leaving them. These represent alternative ways of parsing a constituent. Notice also a new action, exemplified by 'cat det', this action requires that to pass from one node to another, a word of category 'det' must be the next word in the sentence being parsed. If the action is possible the word is stripped from the list of words being analysed.

Transition nets provide an alternative way of representing grammars. The next thing to consider is how to build a program to interpret these networks. Such a program would act as a computational parser.

10.6 Writing a transition net in POP-11

Consider the kinds of action we will need to build into a transition net parser. We will need a procedure to effect the action 'parse', and another to effect the action 'category', and finally a procedure to indicate when constituents are complete. There are two other network characteristics which we will have to represent. One node may have a number of arcs leaving it, and a series of nodes are typically connected together in a network. The first of these features we will treat superficially, we will be implementing a non-backtracking parser which will simply choose an arc at random. The second is trivial to implement, we perform the set of tests connecting nodes in serial order.

There is a natural way of representing transition nets as lists of transition actions, this is shown below. Some of the list elements prefixed by the ^ symbol are procedures (see Section 6.5.3) which we shall build shortly. So you can see that the list contains *actions*: we are to read the list assigned to s_net as a series of consecutive actions, the action parse applied to the value of np_net, followed by the action parse applied to the value of vp_net.

```
define grammar();
[[^choice_pt [[[^category pn]]
                  [[^series [[^category det] [^category noun]]]]]
]]]-> np_net;

[[^choice_pt [[^series [[^category verbt] [^parse ^np_net]]]
                                  [[^category verbi]]]
]] -> vp_net;

[[^series [[^parse ^np_net] [^parse ^vp_net]]
]] -> s_net
enddefine;
```

The lexicon is represented using the database facility.

```
[    [det [the a]]
     [noun [boy girl dog computer]]
     [verbt [loves sees admires]]
     [verbi [walks sleeps cries]]
     [pn [steve ben fiona wendy]]
] -> database;
```

The algorithm we need to interpret the nets is straightforward. The interpreter will simply be a loop which will examine each action in an actions list and apply the appropriate procedure. Each element of the action list will itself be a list whose first element is a procedure and whose second element will be data for the procedure.

If we want to parse the whole sentence the first action to be performed is [^parse ^s_net], so the list of actions at this point will be [[^parse ^s_net]]. This will be interpreted as a call to the procedure parse on the value of s_net. Let us be clear about what these various actions are and what the associated procedures are doing before writing the top level control procedure for the interpreter.

The procedure category takes the head of the input sentence and tests it to see if it is of the appropriate type. If the test succeeds then the word is removed from the head of the sentence, if not a failure is reported. A simple procedure performs this behaviour. Note that our sentence is stored in a global variable input.

```
define category(terminal_symbol);
terminal_symbol =>
if present([^terminal_symbol [== ^(hd(input)) ==]])
then tl(input) -> input
else false -> attempt
endif
enddefine;
```

The action or procedure series simply puts all of the subactions contained in a series of 'linked nodes' onto the front of the actions list.

```
define series(subactions);
[^^subactions] <> actions -> actions
enddefine;
```

The procedure choice_pt will pick one of the alternatives in the list of choices and put it onto the front of the actions list.

```
define choice_pt(choices);
oneof(choices) -> chosen;
ppr([chosen ^chosen]); nl(2);
[^^chosen] <> actions -> actions
enddefine;
```

The procedure parse places a done feature on the front of the actions list and then immediately in front of this action it places the constituent net

to be parsed. The done feature enables the parser to check and detect
when a constituent has been found.

```
define parse(net);
[[^done []]] <> actions -> actions;
net <> actions -> actions
enddefine;
```

When a done procedure is encountered as an action to be performed a
number of checks are required to see if:

1. the list of actions is empty,

2. the input sentence list is empty.

If (1) and (2) are both true then the parser has successfully traversed a
sentence, if (1) is true and (2) is not then the overall parse has failed. If
(1) is false then there are more actions to be tried and the interpreter
should continue examining actions.

```
define done(dummy);
if actions = []
then if input = []
     then true -> attempt
     else false -> attempt
     endif
endif
enddefine;
```

We have provided the procedure done with a dummy argument so that it
has the same action/value structure as all the other action procedures.

We can now build a main procedure for interpreting transition networks. tn_interp sets up a loop through the various actions on the actions
list and iterates through the list.

```
define tn_interp(actions);
vars attempt current_action;

until actions = [] or attempt = false
do hd(actions) -> current_action;
   tl(actions) ->actions;
   current_action(1)(current_action(2))
enduntil;

if attempt = true
then ppr([successful parse]); nl(2)
else ppr([could not parse the sentence]); nl(2)
endif
enddefine;
```

Let us now run the parser on the input sentence 'the boy admires the girl'.

```
: vars input;
: [the boy admires the girl] ->input;
: tn_interp([[^parse ^s_net]]);
** det
** noun
** verbt
** det
** noun
   successful parse
```

So the procedure works – we have broken down the sentence input into its constituent parts.

To follow through in detail the action of the interpreter we will work through an example with a significantly simpler grammar which nevertheless demonstrates the main actions of the parser.

```
define grammar();
[[^choice_pt [[[^category pn]]
                       [[^series [[^category det] [^category noun]]]]
]]]-> np_net;

[[^series [[^parse ^np_net] [^category verbi]]]] -> s_net
enddefine;
```

We will also add an additional line to the tn_interp procedure so that it prints out the list of actions it is using at each stage (i.e. the list actions). If we now run the interpreter on the sentence 'mary cries' the following output is observed.

```
: [mary cries] -> input;
: tn_interp([ [^parse ^s_net] ]);
** [
       [PARSE
           [[SERIES
               [[PARSE
                   [[CHOICE_PT
                       [[[CATEGORY pn]]
                       [[SERIES
                           [[CATEGORY det]
                           [CATEGORY noun]]]]]]]]
                   [CATEGORY verbi]]]]
       ]
   ]
```

(In fact we have represented the output in this form to make it easier to read. If you execute the procedure you will see that PARSE is output as <procedure parse>, and similarly for all procedures.)

At this stage the actions list comprises one action, that of parsing a structure. The structure can be read as saying that to parse a sentence we have to parse a series of nodes which will involve making a choice between ways of parsing a noun phrase and then finding the category 'verbi'. The initial parse action places a done feature on the actions list and then the network representing the s_net is appended to the front of the actions list.

```
**  [
        [SERIES
            [[PARSE
                [[CHOICE_PT
                    [[[CATEGORY pn]]
                    [[SERIES
                        [[CATEGORY det]
                        [CATEGORY noun]]]]]]]]
                [CATEGORY verbi]]]
            [DONE []]
    ]
```

The next action series simply places the sequence of actions, representing the passage along a sequence of nodes, onto the actions list as separate actions.

```
**  [
        [PARSE
            [[CHOICE_PT
                [[[CATEGORY pn]]
                [[SERIES
                    [[CATEGORY det]
                    [CATEGORY noun]]]]]]]
            [CATEGORY verbi]
        [DONE []]
    ]
```

The action parse for an np places a done feature on the actions list and then its relevant network on the actions list

```
**  [
        [CHOICE_PT
            [[[CATEGORY pn]]
                [[SERIES [[CATEGORY det]
                            [CATEGORY noun]]]]]
                [DONE []]
            [CATEGORY verbi]
        [DONE []]
    ]
```

In this case we assume that choice_pt selects the right arc for our example

```
   chosen CATEGORY pn
** [[CATEGORY pn]
   [DONE []]
   [CATEGORY verbi]
   [DONE []]]

** pn
```

We are now down to the action [^category pn] at the top of our actions list. This will succeed, and print out the grammatical constituent found. This amounts to a successful traverse of the np_net, so the done feature placed on the actions list by [^parse np] is now next on the actions list.

```
** [[DONE []]
   [CATEGORY verbi]
   [DONE []]]

** [[CATEGORY verbi]
   [DONE []]]

** verbi

** [[DONE []]]

   successful parse
```

The done feature for np is removed, but the interpreter still has actions to perform. Namely to determine if a word of category 'verb' remains in the input list. This action, in turn, succeeds. Finally, the done feature for the original parse of s_net is encountered. When it is taken off the actions list and executed we discover that that the list of actions is now empty as is the input list. The parse has succeeded.

You should have a good feel for how the transition net interpreter is working. Try some examples of your own with the more extensive grammar. Alternatively you could encapsulate a grammar of your own on a transition net and use it, working on this model.

This interpreter as it stands does not backtrack but can be made to do so very easily. To do this, one only needs to record in an additional list certain variable values when choice points are encountered. Whenever a choice point is encountered record the following pair of values and add them to the front of a list, call it backtrack_options. The first part of the pair is the value of the input sentence at the time the choice is encountered, the other element of the pair consists of the remaining actions on the actions list and one of the alternatives not chosen. Do this for each alternative. Whenever a parse is in danger of failing, look at the backtrack options and take the first pair from the front and make them the new values of input and actions lists. We will leave this as an implementation exercise for the reader.

Transition nets of the sort described here have been used and extended in various ways. A particularly powerful development was the Augmented Transition Network (ATN) devised by Woods (1970). ATNs allow for considerable amounts of information to be recorded on the nodes of networks. This enables us to represent much richer grammars than the simple Phrase Structure Grammars discussed in this chapter. Readers interested in the possibilities of such formalisms should consult Winograd (1983).

Since it is impossible in the space of a single chapter to give more than the briefest descriptions of the various techniques, methods and problems which now define the area of computational linguistics, we have chosen instead to look at a few aspects of one part of the language system. In the next chapter we will mention recent developments in natural language processing – we hope they might, together with this chapter, provide you with a point of departure for further study in the area.

Chapter 11 **Where do we go from here?**

This book was written to consist of two independent but complementary parts. The first was an introduction to an AI programming language, POP-11. The second introduced an activity, AI modelling in POP-11.

This final chapter is divided along similar but more general lines. In the first half we will consider current developments in AI programming languages. The second part of the chapter will look at AI research generally. Finally, we provide some information for readers who want to take their interest in AI and cognitive science further.

11.1 Languages and environments

Interest in AI programming languages is growing fast. Not simply because AI itself has a wider currency. Many 'conventional' software engineers are using AI languages for their own programming problems. They are recognizing the value of the facilities offered by these languages. So let us consider how the languages of AI are faring and what their future is likely to be.

11.1.1 LISP – list based procedural programming

In recent years there has been a lot of discussion about the merits of various languages over one another. Within AI the most popular and widespread language is without doubt LISP. LISP has been around a long time, McCarthy gave the first specification of the language in 1960. What made LISP different from other languages was its orientation toward 'symbolic computation'. LISP was a computer language designed to manipulate non-numeric data structures; the fundamental data structure in LISP is the list. We have seen throughout the second part of this book the power and ubiquity of lists. Lists lie at the heart of a great deal of AI modelling.

By virtue of being first, LISP has accrued a number of advantages over other AI languages. Many of the most famous AI programs and systems were implemented in LISP. Over the years a large number of software tools have been developed to support LISP programming. For example, a variety of powerful editors exist, there is software to enable LISP to run on a wide selection of machines, and so on.

LISP has become the *lingua franca* of the AI community. But because there is such a large community of LISP users we find that 'dialects' have inevitably emerged. These are versions of the language which contain local enhancements and additions. This can result in unwanted 'fragmentation', if the dialect becomes too non-standard it is no longer understood by other users and other machines. The recent emergence of a standard LISP called COMMON LISP is a step back towards unifying the LISP community.

Another important element in the LISP story has been the construction of specialized 'LISP machines'. These are computers whose *hardware* is designed to run the LISP language. By building LISP into the machine hardware we cut out the many levels of software normally required to translate an AI language into the form a normal computer can understand. LISP machines allow large programs to be run very much more quickly than we would find on an ordinary computer which supported the language through 'software translation'. LISP machines make it feasible to construct in LISP certain types of computationally intensive program. The main disadvantage of the current generation of LISP machines is their price. They can cost around $70,000 for the hardware alone.

Contenders to LISP as a general AI programming language are relatively few in number. POP-11 is in some respects a competitor whilst in others it can be seen as complementary. However, we will postpone discussing POP-11 until the end of this section. Let us turn now to consider AI languages which offer different *types* of programming from that of LISP.

11.1.2 PROLOG – logic programming

A language which has aroused much interest lately is PROLOG. PROLOG offers a very different way of programming from LISP, being based on the idea of programming in logic. Languages such as LISP and POP-11 can be characterized as 'procedural'. We build our programs in these languages out of sets of procedures or 'functions' which we have defined. These procedures contain instructions which specify how certain data is to be manipulated and transformed. Thus in procedural languages we explicitly build procedures to do certain computations. Programs in PROLOG, however, consist of sets of assertions of facts and rules of inference; the rules provide ways of inferring new facts from those already given. The PROLOG system then applies its own built in 'inference system' to these facts and rules. A solution to a problem in PROLOG is the result of having the system try to prove a conclusion using the rules and facts supplied.

Logic based programming of the sort found in PROLOG should not be seen as a competitor to list based procedural programming. Rather, it should be seen as complementary – allowing us to program in a style suited to certain classes of problem.

PROLOG was first conceived of by Alan Colmerauer and his colleagues at the University of Marseilles. The principal development work was carried out at the University of Edinburgh by David Warren. PROLOG is now widely used in the international AI community. Its reputation and future were considerably enhanced when it was adopted as the basic research language for the Japanese 'Fifth Generation Computing' project.

PROLOG suffers to some extent because it is a newcomer. There are not, as yet, many software tools to help the PROLOG programmer. The language is not available on a very wide range of machines, and currently there are no commercial 'PROLOG machines'. But all of these obstacles seem set to disappear in the next few years.

11.1.3 SMALLTALK – object oriented programming

Another very different style of programming is embodied in object oriented programming languages. There are a number of languages which support this style of programming. Perhaps the best known of these is the Xerox Corporation's SMALLTALK system (Goldberg & Kay, 1976). In some respects SMALLTALK is best thought of as a *programming environment* rather than a language. Leaving this distinction aside we can say that programs in SMALLTALK consist of a collection of objects which communicate with one another by passing messages. Objects are organized as hierarchies, so that an object can inherit properties from superordinate objects.

The power of SMALLTALK arises from the way it confines procedural computation and data within individual objects. If one object wishes to use information or procedural definitions contained in another object then the former must send a message to the object owning the information or definition. The message must contain all the information necessary to allow the receiving object to generate the required response. The partitioning of programs into objects enforces a strict *modularity* in the way programs are developed. This is generally a desirable property of complex programs.

Object oriented languages are widely used in the area of simulator construction. Consider the domain of Air Traffic Control: one of the things we might wish to do is build a computer model which simulates the behaviour of objects in this domain. This requires that we simulate the properties and behaviours of various aircraft, different kinds of radar and so on. Programs written in, say, SMALLTALK could represent the air traffic domain as SMALLTALK objects that map onto objects in the domain being modelled. Each of the SMALLTALK objects in such a simulation is a discrete and separate entity with its own behaviours. The objects are able to interact with each other via message passing. The modularity of object oriented programs allows new objects to be added to the simulation with a minimum of disruption to earlier versions of the program.

SMALLTALK was originally available only on Xerox machines. However, there now exist versions which run on a range of other computers (these include Sun and Apple Macintosh machines). Interest in object oriented programming continues to grow. As we shall see, it is one of the elements being built into the new generation of 'integrated AI environments'.

11.1.4 OPS5 – production system programming

The last major class of AI programming languages are those that use production system architectures. We met the idea of a production system in Chapter 8. The power of the production system lies in the fact that we can express many types of knowledge as 'rewrite systems' of the following sort:

IF ⟨CONDITION⟩ THEN ⟨ACTION⟩

To use a production system as a complete programming language we need a flexible way of ordering and examining rules. This amounts to providing powerful production system interpreters.

The interpreter we considered in Chapter 8 was very basic. It operated on a 'recognize/act cycle', working from the beginning to the end of a set of rules. One way of extending production systems is to allow for the user to specify different ways of iterating through the rule base. Consider the following control strategies:

1. (a) Examine next rule.
   (b) If it is applicable then fire it.
   (c) If it is the last rule in the rule-set go back to the start of the rule-set.
   (d) Go to (a).

2. (a) Examine next rule.
   (b) If it is applicable then fire it.
   (c) Go back to the start of the rule-set.
   (d) Go to (a).

3. (a) Examine next rule.
   (b) If it is applicable then mark rule.

(c)   If it is the last rule in the rule-set apply technique to select 'best' of marked rules and apply that rule.

(d)   Go to (a).

This is not an exhaustive set of control possibilities. And aspects of those given above remain unspecified, for example, the notion of 'best' rule in (3), or the issue of when the interpreter stops cycling.

Production systems are receiving particular attention at the moment because many of the current generation of 'expert systems' use them. These systems consist of sets of production rules which allow for the construction of rule bases which reflect real-world knowledge.

OPS5 (Forgy, 1981) is one of the most widely used production systems. In addition to a powerful interpreter it has a sophisticated pattern matcher that allows variables to be included in the specification of the productions themselves. It has the added distinction of having been used to implement one of the most oft quoted expert systems, R1. Given a client's requirements R1 decides on the best VAX computer configuration.

As with other programming language types, production systems are an important part of integrated AI environments. It is to these environments we shall now turn.

11.1.5 Integrated environments

An interesting recent development in AI software is the move away from 'language imperialism' – the view that one AI language is the best one to use in all circumstances. This has come about, in part, because of the emergence of systems such as POPLOG. These systems offer a wide range of utilities to the AI program writer. The environments, written in a base language, offer the user a number of programming methodologies and a number of support tools. Thus in POPLOG (which is written in POP-11) we can call up POP-11 itself, PROLOG or COMMON LISP. POPLOG offers a powerful editor so that we can construct program files – these are collections of programming instructions stored in the computer. POPLOG also has large collections of on-line teaching files, on-line documentation, and a large set of 'library programs' (programs to do useful computations and which the user can 'plug' into his own programs). An additional feature of POPLOG and some other integrated environments is the ability to have a POP-11 program call a program written in another language. So if there were a lot of numerical computations to do we might call upon some FORTRAN programs from within our POP-11 code. The arrival of such environments allows programmers to write the majority of their code in the language best suited to the problem requirements.

Another advantage of the high level environment in the hands of an experienced programmer is the speed with which programs can be developed. This is sometimes referred to as **rapid prototyping**. A putative solution is constructed. It is then written as a program using an editor. Sections of the emerging program can be loaded into the system and tested to see if they work. We can then see the results of parts of the program, trace various procedures, log these traces, move back into the editor environment, look at the code and the output traces, and modify our code if necessary.

As indicated POPLOG is one of a number of such integrated environments. Others include KEE, LOOPS, LOGLISP and ART. Each offers different facilities but the general idea behind them is the same. Thus KEE offers programming in LISP, a logic programming environment, a production system capability as well as editing and debugging tools. LOOPS contains LISP, object oriented programming, logic programming and a production system together with other support software.

In many ways POPLOG as a *programming environment* may do more to secure a healthy future for POP-11 than any particular feature of POP-11 itself. POPLOG runs on a number of machines popular in the AI community. In comparison with many of the American environments the commercial licence is relatively cheap. Moreover the latest versions are considerably more efficient and comprehensive than was previously the case. An additional feature is the large amount of AI tutorial and teaching material supplied with the system.

11.1.6 Expert system shells

Interest in expert systems has led to the development of a number of so-called 'expert system shells'. Commercially available shells include SAGE, SAVOIR, REVEAL, ESP ADVISOR and Xi. They range in price from a few hundred to many thousands of pounds. These software packages are sold as *aids* to expert system construction. The idea behind these shells is that we can strip the 'domain dependent knowledge' from out of a standard expert system. This leaves behind a **shell** which consists of the original system's reasoning component and knowledge representation formalism. Usually we are left with some form of production system.

In practice, experienced programmers find shells restrictive to use, whilst clients often find that the problems they would like their expert systems to solve are much more difficult than current shells can cope with. In our experience the best shell is a high level programming language! And in fact as shells become more sophisticated it will become harder to differentiate them from the sort of integrated programming environment discussed in the previous section.

11.1.7 AI workstations

Associated with developments in software there have been considerable advances in hardware. We have already described the arrival on the scene of 'AI machines'. Another development is the emergence of 'AI workstations'.

The term AI workstation is something of a misnomer. The kind of machine being offered under this title could just as well be used in a wide variety of other applications, for example, in computer aided design (CAD). Also, whilst some of these workstations are hardware LISP machines, not all of them are.

AI workstations have evolved to fulfill the AI researcher's needs; their languages and programs are greedy both in terms of the memory needed to store them and the time taken to process them. Typically, computer users find themselves sharing the computer with other users, these time-sharing systems allocate limited amounts of memory and processing time to each user in turn. Although a large number of users may be logged on to the machine at the same time, and it may look as if they have the machine to themselves, this is not the case. The computer is attending to each of them for a short while before going on to the next. This usually happens so fast that the users do not 'feel' the presence of the other users on the computer. Put an AI user on the system and things are apt to change – AI programs often slow the whole system down.

The drop in the cost of computer hardware, and the development of more powerful 'chips', have made it possible to design powerful single user workstations. These are systems with the following features:

- Each user has unique access to one computer.
- Each computer has a large memory.
- Each computer has a fast processing cycle.
- The computer is provided with high resolution terminals with graphical interfaces.
- Networks of these computers are linked and able to communicate with each other.
- Each computer is able to run integrated programming environments.

The advent of such systems promises a most congenial working environment!

11.2 AI – current and future trends

Anyone associated with AI over the past decade will have witnessed a dramatic change in attitudes and interest towards the subject. AI now generates enough heat and light to persuade even the most cautious that it has arrived!

There are those who argue that this is simply the latest in a series of infatuations with the subject, and that in a year or so it will sink once more into peaceful obscurity. There are reasons to believe that whilst the current level of excitement may abate, AI is well and truly here to stay.

Why has AI so suddenly come to the fore? Has the public imagination been gripped by the idea of creating 'artificial minds'? We would argue that the current interest is due to a number of factors: technical, political, and commercial.

In some respects AI has been its own worst enemy. In the past it tended to promote its most outrageous claims at the expense of its real achievements. The substantial advances that AI has made in the areas of software and hardware, and in the provision of a set of basic research techniques have tended to be overshadowed by the Messianic claims of some of its practitioners. One way of viewing AI is to see it as the 'leading edge' of certain sorts of computer science. Within this perspective what was yesterday's intelligent system becomes today's conventional software.

Aside from the technical advances which AI has made the subject has also received considerable political attention. This political interest has had considerable practical consequences. In the UK the Government set up the ALVEY Directorate – this has provided considerable funding for industrial and academic research in the areas of software engineering, man/machine interfaces, intelligent knowledge based systems, and very large scale integration (VLSI – chip design and manufacture). France and the USA have similar national research programmes, and the EEC has its own international programme of research into advanced information technology called ESPRIT.

It is fair to say that many of these national programmes were stimulated by the fear that the equivalent Japanese program, ICOT, would give Japan an even bigger share of the world's computer markets.

These various programmes have ensured AI a healthy future in terms of funding levels. Much of this research will be directed to what we might term 'non-cognitive AI'. Whilst this type of AI aims to provide solutions which would require intelligence to solve if they were attempted by humans, there is no requirement that 'non-cognitive AI' solutions should correspond in any way, manner or means to those processes a human might use in solving the problem.

In contrast the type of AI modelling we have talked about in this book has been concerned to provide insights into human cognitive processes. Has AI provided us with a conceptual revolution in our understanding of 'cognitive processes'? It would be foolish to claim that it has. But there has been a considerable amount of work in AI that is relevant to scholars in the other cognitive sciences of psychology, linguistics and philosophy. The problem has been one of communication – work in AI needs to be disseminated to those who might benefit from it in other areas of cognitive science. The problem has been exacerbated by a lack of good AI texts, demonstration software and the like. However, it looks as if this is changing and it is to be hoped that researchers and students from other disciplines will be able to assess the relevance of AI work to their own work whilst at the same time feeding their own ideas back into AI.

To illustrate the wealth of research around in AI let us consider again the four main areas of cognitive modelling dealt with in this book. For each of these areas we can find research work which demonstrates the rapid development of the field in the last few years.

11.2.1 Advances in problem solving

The basic techniques of searching problem and state spaces are now well established. (Nilsson (1982) provides an excellent account of the details of these techniques.) Many of these techniques include the use of 'heuristic information' and 'pruning algorithms' – these allow the search to be concentrated only in those parts of the search space most likely to yield a solution.

Within the context of problem solving programs there have been attempts to have programs transfer learning from one problem domain to another, other programs acquire problem solving expertise during repeated exposure to the same problem. Learning programs can be distinguished in terms of the underlying learning strategy. We find examples of AI systems which exhibit:

- learning from instruction (Hass & Hendrix, 1984; Ryechner, 1984);
- learning by analogy (Anderson, 1984);
- learning from examples (Winston, 1975);
- learning from observation and discovery (Lenat, 1982).

In all cases learning can be regarded as a special sort of problem solving behaviour; in some cases, such as the work by Lenat, learning is dependent on some sort of antecedent problem solving having taken place. The relevance of this sort of work to cognitive psychology hardly needs emphasizing.

The performance of human experts when solving problems in their specialist domains is just another type of problem solving. The work on expert systems within AI has produced results in the following areas:

- knowledge elicitation techniques (Welbank, 1983);
- representing and reasoning with uncertain and inconsistent knowledge (Reiter, 1978; McDermott & Doyle, 1980);
- presenting explanations of a system's reasoning (Swartout, 1983).

All of this research is of potential interest to anyone seeking insights into the types of processing model that we might propose for the cognitive activities we label as 'problem solving'.

11.2.2 Advances in knowledge representation

In Chapter 8 we considered the proposals of Collins and Quillian for semantic memory. Other work in AI has attempted to construct models of human memory. Minsky (1979) has proposed the idea of 'K-Lines' as a theory of memory. A K-Line induces a partial state resembling the one that created it. A partial state is a subset of those processes operating at any one moment. This is meant to provide a retrieval mechanism that is at once powerful and open to error. As Minsky points out it is necessary in any model of human memory to be able to account for forgetting as well as remembering.

In a broader context AI has furnished a wide range of 'knowledge representation formalisms'. These include Minsky's Frame System (1975), Schank's Scripts (Schank and Abelson, 1977) and Anderson's Semantic Associative Memories (Anderson and Bower, 1973). Whilst no one believes that the 'language of thought' has been revealed, what we do have is a number of ways of thinking about the issue of knowledge representation.

11.2.3 Advances in planning

Since the early days of STRIPS a great deal of work has gone into the area of planning. There now exist a number of different methods and techniques for: representing plans and their constituents, reasoning about plans, executing and monitoring plans, repairing plans, and so forth. The research mentioned below is only a part of the picture.

One area that has been studied in detail is the problem of constructing planning systems which are able to detect interactions between sub-plans. In Chapter 9 we discovered how in simple planning we can sometimes perform actions whilst achieving a sub-goal, which undo a goal achieved in an earlier part of the planning process. 'Hierarchical Planners' (Sacerdoti, 1974) check that a plan is feasible at a general level before dealing with the details of the plan.

Another area of research has looked at 'backing up' intelligently on failure. If a plan is constructed for a goal and it turns out that part of the plan cannot be carried out in the way first proposed then the planner ought to be able to remake choices intelligently about other ways of achieving the goal. To do this means keeping records of the reasons why certain choices were made. These systems are now under development, *cf.* for example, the TEAMWORK system (Doran, 1985).

An area of considerable interest to the cognitive scientist is the use of meta-knowledge in planning. Planning may be more effective if it is able to use 'knowledge about planning'. The explicit use of knowledge about the control of planning and of the resources available to the planner can be used to influence planning behaviour. The use of planning meta-knowledge can be found in systems such as MOLGEN (Stefik, 1981).

11.2.4 Advances in natural language processing

Work in computational linguistics has been progressing from the outset of research into AI. Much of it is of potential interest to the psycho-linguist. For example, Berwick (in press) has been investigating how systems can be built that are able to extract the grammar of a language given examples of sentences of the language.

Work has continued in the area of syntactic parsing, many alternative parsing mechanisms now exist (*cf.* for example ATNS (Woods, 1970), Deterministic Parsers (Marcus, 1979; Milne, 1982)). Moreover strong claims have been made about the psychological reality of these various systems (Wanner & Maratsos, 1978; Wanner, 1980; Milne, 1982).

Research has begun to make headway in the area of machine understanding of dialogue and discourse structure. The aim is to extend the knowledge a machine can have about linguistic structure beyond that of the sentence (*cf.* for example Webber, 1983; Sidner, 1983). Work has been done on implementing focus mechanisms, providing systems with the ability to recognize when changes of topic have occurred, and how old topics are taken up again (Grosz, 1978).

Finally Allen (1983) has investigated natural language understanding in terms of plan based activity. He has recast speech act theory (Searle, 1969) as a computational theory of planning. In this account the various preparatory conditions of speech acts are seen as equivalent to the preconditions to be fulfilled in a plan. Utterances are seen as the surface realization of plans. This AI work, using as it does a theory of interest to psychologists, linguists and philosophers, demonstrates once again the degree to which researchers in all the disciplines of cognitive science stand to gain from closer study of each other's work.

11.3 Where should you go from here?

If your interest in cognitive modelling and AI has been whetted then there are a number of books, journals, conferences and organizations that might be of interest to you.

Starting with POP-11 itself, apart from the material contained within the POPLOG system, there is one other book we know of which deals with POP-11. This is

> Barrett, R., Ramsay, A. and Sloman, A. (1985). *POP-11 A Practical Language for Artificial Intelligence*. Chichester: Ellis Horwood.

This book deals in more detail than we have with the data and control structures of POP-11. However, the book does not contain any substantial worked AI examples.

For those of you in a position to obtain or influence the purchase of a POPLOG system then, if you are a non-academic site, you should contact:

Systems Designers Ltd,
1 Pembroke Broadway,
Camberley, Surrey,
England, GU15 3XH

If you are a recognized academic site, contact:

Cognitive Studies Programme,
Arts Building E,
University of Sussex,
Brighton,
England, BN1 9QN

There also exists a POPLOG user group which is organized by:

Martin Bennett,
Cambridge Consultants Ltd,
Science Park,
Milton Road,
Cambridge,
England, CB4 4DW

This publishes a newsletter, organizes meetings and conferences.

There has recently been a welcome influx of AI titles into publishers' lists. Some good general introductory texts to AI now exist:

Winston, P. H. (1984). *Artificial Intelligence*. Addison-Wesley. 2nd Edition.

Charniak, E. and McDermott, D. (1985). *Introduction to Artificial Intelligence*. Addison-Wesley.

Rich, E. (1983). *Artificial Intelligence*. McGraw-Hill.

Barr, A. and Feigenbaum, E. A.; Eds (1981). *The Handbook of Artificial Intelligence Vols I, II, III*. Addison-Wesley.

These will also serve as good sources for references to more specialist texts. Two textbooks that deal with the conceptual issues surrounding the area of cognitive and AI modelling are:

Plyshyn, Z. W. (1984). *Computation and Cognition: Toward a Foundation for Cognitive Science*. MIT Press.

Sowa, J. F. (1984). *Conceptual Structures: Information Processing in Mind and Machine*. Addison-Wesley.

If you are interested in looking at any of the other AI languages mentioned in this chapter then the following are amongst the best, and in some cases only, available texts:

LISP

Winston, P. H. and Horn, B. K. P. (1984). *LISP*. Addison-Wesley.

PROLOG

Clocksin, W. F. and Mellish, C. S. (1981). *Programming in Prolog*. Springer-Verlag.

SMALLTALK

Goldberg, A. and Robson, D. (1983). *Smalltalk-80: The Language and its Implementation*. Addison-Wesley.

OPS5

Brownston, L., Farrell, R., Kant, E. and Martin, N. (1985). *Programming Expert Systems in OPS5*. Addison-Wesley.

Journals that may be of interest include *Artificial Intelligence* and the journal of the American Cognitive Science Society entitled *Cognitive Science*. In addition there are a number of societies to which you can subscribe. Chief amongst these are The Society for the Study of Artificial Intelligence and the Simulation of Behaviour (SSAISB). This is the UK AI society and it publishes a quarterly newsletter and organizes a biennial conference. SSAISB is affiliated, along with other European AI groups, to ECCAI – the European Coordinating Committee for Artificial Intelligence. This distributes a newsletter via its national member organizations and also puts on a biannual European AI conference. The British Computer Society has a number of specialist groups with AI interests. The most AI oriented is the Specialist Group on Expert Systems which distributes a newsletter and organizes a national annual conference. There are a number of American organizations which one is free to subscribe to, the most notable of which is the American Association for Artificial Intelligence (AAAI). This produces a quarterly magazine and organizes an annual conference. The major international conference on AI is held every two years, this is IJCAI (International Joint Congress on Artificial Intelligence). The addresses of these various organizations are provided at the end of the book.

In conclusion we hope you have found the material in this book useful and interesting. The future for POP-11 as a language and AI as a discipline looks to be an exciting one.

Appendix A **Solutions to Selected Exercises**

The solutions offered in this appendix should be regarded as suggestions. There are usually many different ways to write a program to perform the same task, and it may be that your answers are just as good as the ones given here.

The solutions are constrained to use only those techniques introduced before the exercises. So, for example, there are better (easier) ways to solve the problems given in Chapter 4, but these are not introduced until Chapter 5. You might like to re-write some of the solutions offered here with the benefit of hindsight, after you have read the whole book.

Chapter 2

1. 3

2. [4 5]

3. 3

4. 4

5. 2

8. [The days of the week are ^(rev(tl(rev(weekdays))))
and ^(hd(rev(weekdays)))] =>

Chapter 3

1. define last_two(lista);
hd(rev(lista)) =>
hd(tl(rev(lista))) =>
enddefine;

2. define last_el(listb);
vars len;
length(listb) -> len;
listb(len) =>
enddefine;

```
3. define prod_mean(n1,n2,n3);
   vars prod;
   n1*n2*n3 -> prod;
   prod =>
   prod/3 =>
   enddefine;
```

Chapter 4

```
1. define all_caps(countries);
   if countries = []
   then
   else capital(hd(countries)) =>
        all_caps(tl(countries))
   endif
   enddefine;
```

```
2. define count(el,list);
   vars n; 0 -> n;
   until list = []
   do  if hd(list) = el
       then n+1 -> n
       endif;
       tl(list) -> list
   enduntil;
   n =>
   enddefine;
```

```
3. define common(lista,listb);
   vars tempb; listb -> tempb;
   until lista = []
   do  until tempb = []
       do  if hd(lista) = hd(tempb)
           then hd(lista) =>
           endif;
           tl(tempb) -> tempb
       enduntil;
       listb -> tempb;
       tl(lista) -> lista
   enduntil
   enddefine;
```

```
4. define mean(nums);
   vars tot; 0-> tot;
   until nums = []
   do  tot+hd(nums) -> tot;
       tl(nums) -> nums
```

```
enduntil;
tot =>
enddefine;
```

Chapter 5

We use the procedure getrid as defined in Section 5.1

```
1. define uncommon(lista,listb);
   vars tempb; listb -> tempb;
   until tempb = []
   do  if lista matches [== ^(hd(tempb)) ==]
       then getrid(hd(tempb),lista) -> lista;
            getrid(hd(tempb),listb) -> listb;
       endif;
       tl(tempb) -> tempb
   enduntil;
   lista =>
   listb =>
   enddefine;
2. define alternate(list);
   if length(list) < 2
   then
   else hd(list) =>
        alternate(tl(tl(list)))
   endif
   enddefine;
```

Note the different stopping condition in this example.

Appendix B **Addresses of AI Associations and Societies**

Society for the Study of Artificial Intelligence and the Simulation of Behaviour

Membership Secretary,
Judith Dennison,
SSAISB,
Cognitive Studies Programme,
Arts Building,
University of Sussex,
Brighton,
England, BN1 9QN

The American Association for Artificial Intelligence

Membership,
AAAI,
445 Burgess Drive,
Menlo Park,
California 94025-3496

The British Computer Society Specialist Group on Expert Systems

Secretary,
Mr Maurice Ashill,
The Grange Cottage,
Off Southborough Road,
Surbiton,
Surrey,
England

Appendix C The POPLOG Programming Environment

In Chapter 11 we described the recent emergence of integrated programming environments. This is software that, as a package, offers a wide range of facilities. POPLOG is such an environment.

It is impossible to give a comprehensive account of how to get started in POPLOG. We can, at least, describe how to get into POPLOG, and where to start looking for information on the system. When we first login to a computer supporting the POPLOG system we will typically find ourselves at the level of the operating system. This is a software application that allocates time and memory to various users of a computer and also allows you to call up other applications. You can usually tell where you are in a system because the system components present you with different prompts. Two of the most common prompts to appear at the beginning of a line on a terminal when you are at the operating system level are shown below.

```
$

%
```

Which one you see will depend on the particular operating system your computer is using. To move into POPLOG it is usual to give the operating system a command such as

```
% poplog
```

--- prints a welcome message

```
Setpop
:
```

After typing the appropriate command (this may vary from installation to installation – check with your computer manager) you will get a message from the POPLOG system and then find yourself in the POP-11 language area, indicated by the colon prompt. You can now start typing in POP-11 instructions.

When using any integrated programming environment you need to be sure where you are in the system, what various components there are and what they do. Figure C.1 indicates the main components of POPLOG.

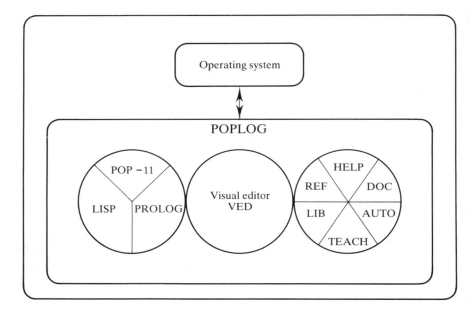

Figure C.1 Main components of POPLOG.

POPLOG contains three different languages in which we can write programs. These are POP-11, LISP and PROLOG. You should be well
versed in the first by now, and we have discussed the general properties of
LISP and PROLOG in Chapter 11. You can get to any of the languages
from the operating system level or from any of the other languages.

POPLOG also provides us with a very powerful editor. An editor is a
powerful tool in any programming environment since it allows you to
construct 'files'. Files can contain any kind of information – a useful file
would be one which stored POP-11 programming instructions. You could
save these files, modify them or remove them as you saw fit. You could
also read them into the POP-11 system as required.

Finally POPLOG contains a huge number of files holding information
on the system. The files of interest to us can be subdivided into six major
types. These are TEACH files, HELP files, REF (reference) files, DOC
(documentation) files, AUTO (auto-loadable) files and LIB (library) files.

TEACH files provide tutorial information about AI techniques in general and features of the POPLOG environment in particular. They also
contain advice on what other files provide additional and supplementary
material on the topic contained in the current file. There is, therefore, a
degree of cross-referencing between files but this does not amount to a
structured course on any particular topic. The problem when faced with
POPLOG's large number of on-line files is to find a place to start.

Perhaps, the best advice is to issue the command shown below from within POP-11.

```
: teach teachfiles
```

The command teach uses the editor VED to display the relevant file, in this case TEACHFILES which gives a brief overview of the various contents of the teach files. These include files on how to use the VED editor.

HELP files provide specific help and information on the constructs of the various programming languages. There are numerous files on the bits and pieces that make up POP-11. Again a command help followed by the name of a help file will use the VED editor to display the contents of the files. Try help contents for an overview of the HELP files available on your system.

REF (reference) files and DOC (documentation) files contain very detailed and definitive explanations of the various language constructs, along with information about how they are implemented on the computer. If you type ref index or doc index you will be shown a list of the files available under these headings.

LIB (library) files contain already written POP-11, and other language, programs that allow you to run various AI algorithms. They effectively constitute a suite of 'built in' programs. The documentation associated with these programs is found in the HELP and TEACH files.

Finally, the AUTO (auto-loadable) files are additional 'built-in' programs that are loaded automatically on entry into various components of the POPLOG system and support such things as the VED editor.

From within the POPLOG environment any component can be reached from any other. All files can be read using VED. Programs written in any of the languages can be written in files using VED and then given over to the particular language to interpret them as sets of program instructions.

From this very brief description we can begin to see the rich and powerful facilities that an integrated programming environment can offer.

Glossary of Terms

Algorithm A formal specification for solving a problem. An algorithm is guaranteed to find a solution – this contrasts with a *heuristic*.

And/Or tree A tree structure (usually representing a search space) designed such that some branches have to be searched in conjunction with each other, while others are alternatives. See p. 130.

Arc A link connecting two nodes in a network. See p. 106.

Argument The data provided to a procedure. When defining a procedure this data is represented as a variable. Procedures in POP-11 can have any number of arguments. See p. 24.

Array An *n*-dimensional data object. Arrays are created using the POP-11 procedure newarray. See p. 75.

Artificial intelligence The attempt to write programs which will enable machines to perform tasks which would require intelligence if performed by humans.

Backtracking The technique of undoing behaviour which has led to an unsatisfactory outcome. This is often needed when a branch of a problem space has been exhausted without finding a solution. See p. 97.

Backwards search A search technique in which one (a) starts with the goal state and applies the transformation rules in reverse until one reaches the start state, or (b) applies a problem reduction operator until only primitive problems remain. See p. 129.

Best-first search A search technique in which the choice of route is determined by measuring the closeness of each option to the goal. The closest state is then expanded. See p. 103.

Bottom up programming A way of writing programs in which the lowest level 'nuts and bolts' procedures are written first. The program is built as a collection of elements.

Closed world An artificial world which a modeller specifies as the domain for the model. Closed worlds have an enumerable number of states and a fixed set of ways in which the world may be transformed. It is obviously much simpler to construct closed worlds for models than to try to model the real world – where any number of things might happen. See p. 2.

Cognitive modelling The term given to the process of constructing models of human cognitive capacities, examples of which are vision, natural language understanding and human problem solving. When engaged in cognitive modelling, one is constrained to build into the model only those features which do not contradict what is known about human cognition. See p. 10.

Connective A relation between two statements in a logic, used to construct a complex statement. Examples of connectives are AND, OR, etc. See p. 119.

Control structure This determines the way in which information flows through a program. Examples of built in facilities for designing the control structure of POP-11 programs are iterative loops and conditionals.

Depth-first search A search technique in which the set of transformation rules is tried in order until an applicable rule is found. Once this rule is applied, the process starts again. From any state the rule nearest the front of the rule-set is always tried first, regardless of whether this is likely to lead to an early solution or not. See p. 87.

Editor A computer program for creating and modifying files. The POPLOG environment comes with the editor VED. Other systems have their own editors.

Execution Making a program work. Once a procedure has been defined, it can be executed whenever it is needed. This is also called *calling* a procedure.

Expert system A specialized problem solving program designed to work in a single area of human expertise. Expert systems typically work on real-world problems, as contrasted with constrained artificial problems such as the Tower of Hanoi. See pp. 180, 181.

File A store of information on a computer. Files may contain text or programs, and are created and modified using an editor.

Formal model A model in which one has been very precise about how its elements fit together. Formal models are usually constructed from formal modelling mediums, like mathematics or a programming language. See p. 6.

Format The design of output from programs. See p. 74.

Functional model A model which represents a process rather than an object. See p. 5.

General Problem Solver (GPS) An early AI program written by Newell and Simon. The program uses the technique of means-ends analysis to solve problems in any domain which can be expressed in terms of goals and operators. See pp. 83, 134.

Goal stack A push-down stack used for storing goals in the STRIPS formalism. See p. 135.

Goal-directed search Another name for backwards search.

Grammar rule A rule which defines legal combinations of syntax elements for parsing and sentence generation.

Heuristic A rule of thumb which aids solution to some problem. A heuristic does not necessarily guarantee a solution (an *algorithm* does this). Heuristics are used to guide search in some way and hence cut down the amount of search required.

Heuristic function A way of measuring closeness-to-solution for use in a best-first search. The measurement is usually based on a heuristic, hence its name. See p. 103.

Implementation The coding of a set of instructions in a programming language.

Inheritance A feature of a semantic net which allows nodes to inherit properties associated with superordinate nodes. This saves on space as the properties associated with high level nodes do not have to be stored explicitly for each subordinate node. See p. 108.

Interactive A mode of communication with a computer such that data can be entered directly from a terminal, and output is immediate. This contrasts with the style of communication in which complete information has to be entered into a queue and output comes some time later. By analogy, interactive communication is like talking to someone on the telephone as opposed to communicating by letters.

Interface The place where two systems meet. This term is often used to mean the human/computer interface, i.e. what the human actually sees as a result of a program.

Iteration A technique for controlling flow in a program. A *loop* is set up so that the same set of instructions is applied repeatedly until some stopping condition is met. Examples of iterative facilities in POP-11 are until loops and foreach loops. See p. 43.

Knowledge representation The issue of how to represent knowledge in a formal system. Examples of techniques available for knowledge representation are semantic nets and production systems. See p. 106.

LISP A list processing computer language which is popular in AI. See pp. 10, 176.

List An ordered set of elements. A list is an important data object in several AI languages as it provides a convenient way of representing the structures AI programmers typically want to manipulate. Lists in POP-11 are enclosed in square brackets. See p. 16.

Logging in The process of identifying yourself to the computer. Once the machine has identified you as a legal user, it will allow you access to the appropriate facilities.

Logic A formal system for representing and manipulating information. Logic has been used in several knowledge representation techniques. See p. 118.

Loop A set of instructions which is performed repeatedly until some stopping condition is met, see *iteration*.

Means-ends analysis A problem solving technique which operates by extracting differences between the goal state and the current state of some problem world. Once the differences are extracted, an attempt is made to reduce them by means of a set of operators. This is the problem solving technique used in GPS. See pp. 105, 135.

Mishap An error from the POP-11 system which tells you that you have tried to do something which is not permitted in the language.

Natural language A language which humans use to communicate with one another and which has evolved naturally. Examples of natural languages are English and French. These contrast with artificial human languages like Esperanto, and with programming languages like POP-11.

Node An element in a *semantic net*. These are connected by *arcs*. See p. 106.

Non-linear search A search technique which combines forward and backwards search.

Number A data object in POP-11 which corresponds to the everyday meaning of number, i.e. it can be used with +, -, etc.

Numbered access A way of accessing elements in a list by specifying their position in the list. See p. 22.

Operator A way of changing the world in a problem domain. These are used in conjunction with a program to apply them in a systematic way, for example in means-ends analysis. See p. 130.

Output local A local variable which is declared in the first line of a procedure definition. Each time the procedure is executed, the value of this variable is left on the stack. See p. 51.

Parsing The process of dividing a statement into its constituent syntactic parts.

Pattern matching The technique in which a complete set of data (e.g. a list) is matched against a template, or skeleton set. Pattern matching in POP-11 is done using the `matches` operator. See p. 53.

Phrase Structure Grammar A system for the analysis or generation of a sentence. Phrase Structure Grammars provide *grammar rules* for breaking the sentence down into phrases, and for breaking the phrases down into elements. There is also a lexicon which associates the elements with actual words. See p. 153.

Planning A specialized form of problem solving in which the aim is to produce a *plan* for action rather than actually to perform manipulations in the world. See p. 131.

POP-11 A high level programming language for AI.

POPLOG A programming environment which includes POP-11, PROLOG, LISP, an editor – VED – and on-line documentation at several levels. Almost all users of POP-11 access the language through the POPLOG system.

Predicate calculus A formal logic in which statements are formed by providing *arguments* to *predicates*. For example 'is_town(London)' is a statement in predicate calculus. See p. 118.

Problem reduction A technique used in problem solving whereby large problems are broken down into sets of smaller, more manageable problems. See p. 130.

Problem space The set of all possible states which your problem world can be in. This space is searched in problem solving. The space is also called the *state space*. See p. 85.

Production rule A statement of the form

IF ⟨CONDITION⟩ THEN ⟨ACTION⟩

Production system A set of *production rules* plus a program for making them work in a systematic way. Production systems provide a way of representing knowledge, and are often used as the basis for expert systems. See p. 120.

Programming environment A set of computer programs which, in conjunction, facilitate the development of programs. Programming environments typically contain one or more programming languages, an editor and lots of easily accessible documentation. See p. 180.

Programming language A specialized language for giving instructions to a computer.

Prompt A symbol, or set of symbols, which tells you that the computer is ready to receive instructions. In POP-11 the colon (:) is used as a prompt.

Property table A table of item/value associations. In POP-11 you can make these associations using `newassoc`. Property tables provide an efficient way of associating items with values. See p. 80.

Quantifier A term from logic specifying the range that a variable has for any given statement. See p. 119.

Record class A type of data object. In POP-11 you can add to the existing set of record classes using `recordclass`. See p. 78.

Recursion A programming technique in which a procedure definition includes a call to that procedure. Recursion is an alternative to iteration for applying one set of instructions many times. It also provides a powerful way of modelling certain problems. See p. 39.

Reserved word A word in POP-11 which has a fixed meaning, e.g. hd and define. You may not re-define these words by creating variables or procedures with the same name.

Scope The range in which a variable has its value. The primary distinction is between local and global variables. Global variables may be accessed at any time, whereas local variables may be accessed only inside the procedure in which they are declared and any procedures called by that procedure.

Search space That part of a *problem space* which is searched by a problem solving program.

Semantic net A knowledge representation device in which *nodes* are connected by *arcs*. The nodes represent elements in the world you are representing, whereas the arcs represent relations between the nodes. See p. 106.

Semantics The *meaning* of a statement in a language (real or artificial). This contrasts with the *syntax* of a statement.

Slot-and-filler A notation for representing data structures in a program. Each structure has a fixed number of *slots* representing characteristics of the structure. Each of these slots is *filled* with a particular value. Slot-and-filler notation is often used to represent nodes in a semantic net or frames in a frame system.

Stack A push-down structure in POP-11 on which data is put. This can be used to leave information from one procedure which another procedure will then pick up. The important thing to remember about the POP-11 stack is that it works on a 'last-on is first-off' principle. See p. 27.

State space See *problem space*.

Statement A complete instruction. Statements are separated by semi-colons in POP-11. See p. 50.

Stopping condition A condition under which recursive or iterative runs are halted. It is important to set an appropriate stopping condition when programming using these structures, otherwise computations tend to go on for ever. See p. 39.

String A data object in POP-11 comprising a set of characters enclosed in single quotes. Strings are most often used in formatting. See p. 74.

STRIPS A device for representing operations in planning. STRIPS specifies how to represent start states, goal states and operators. See p. 135.

Structural model A model which represents how some object is constructed rather than being a representation of what it does. See p. 5.

Syntax The formal rules for constructing legal statements in a language. Natural languages have a syntax (or grammar) as do programming languages. The syntax of POP-11 tells you what is and is not permissible in the language.

Template A partial specification of some structure which is used to match real data against. See p. 54.

Top down programming A way of programming in which the overall control programs are written first. The 'nuts-and-bolts' programs are written so that they fit into the overall structure.

Transformation rule A rule for transforming one state into another in a problem world. Most problems have a specified set of transformation rules (e.g. the Tower of Hanoi problem).

Transition network A way of describing a set of grammar rules in semantic network notation. In this scheme, elements of a grammar are represented as nodes, and legal transformations as arcs. The technique is used most commonly in sentence parsing. See p. 164.

Updater A mechanism for changing the elements in a data structure by using procedures which normally access the data structure. For example, hd can be used to change the head of a list, as well as to find out what the head is. The means by which this is done is called an updater. See p. 72.

Variable A data structure in POP-11 which takes the value of some other structure. If we have a variable called X, we can arrange for X to have any value we like, whether number, list, word, procedure or whatever. See p. 18.

VED The editor which comes with POPLOG.

Word A data object in POP-11 which is formed by enclosing a set of characters in double quotation marks. See p. 16.

Bibliography

Allen, J. F. (1983). 'Recognizing Intentions from Natural Language Utterances' In Brady, M. and Berwick, R. C.; Eds. *Computational Models of Discourse*. Cambridge, Mass: MIT Press

Anderson, J. R. (1984). 'Acquisition of Proof Skills in Geometry' In Michalski, R. S., Carbonell, J. G. and Mitchell, T. M.; Eds. *Machine Learning*. New York: Springer-Verlag

Anderson, J. R. and Bower, G. H. (1973). *Human Associative Memory*. Washington DC: Winston

Barr, A. and Feigenbaum, E. A. (1981). *The Handbook of Artificial Intelligence*. Reading, Mass: Addison-Wesley

Barrett, R., Ramsay, A. and Sloman, A. (1985). *POP-11: A Practical Language for Artificial Intelligence*. Chichester: Ellis Horwood Ltd

Berwick, R. (In press). *The Acquisition of Syntactic Knowledge*. Cambridge Mass: MIT Press

Brownston, L., Farrell, R., Kant, E. and Martin, N. (1985). *Programming Expert Systems in OPS5*. Reading, Mass: Addison-Wesley

Charniak, E. and McDermott, D. (1985). *Introduction to Artificial Intelligence*. Wokingham: Addison-Wesley

Clocksin, W. and Mellish, C. (1981). *Programming in PROLOG*. New York: Springer-Verlag

Collins, A. M. and Quillian, M. R. (1969). 'Retrieval Time from Semantic Memory' *Journal of Verbal Learning and Verbal Behaviour*, **8**, 240–248

Doran, J. (1985). 'The Computational Approach to Knowledge, Communication and Structure in Multi-actor Systems' In Gilbert, E. G. and Heath, C.; Eds. *Social Action and Artificial Intelligence*. London: Gower Press

Duda, R. O., Gasching, J. G. and Hart, P. E. (1979). Model Design in the PROSPECTOR Consultant System for Mineral Exploration' In Michie, D.; Ed. *Expert Systems in the Micro-Electronic Age*. Edinburgh: Edinburgh University Press

Ernst, G. and Newell, A. (1969). *GPS: A Case Study in Generality and Problem Solving*. New York: Academic Press

Evans, T. G. (1968). 'A Program for the Solution of Geometric-Analogy Intelligence Test Questions' In Minsky, M. L.; Ed. *Semantic Information Processing*. Cambridge, Mass: MIT Press

Eysenck, M. W. (1984). *A Handbook of Cognitive Psychology*. London: Lawrence Erlbaum

Fikes, R. E. and Nilsson, N. J. (1971). 'STRIPS: A New Approach to the Application of Theorem Proving to Problem Solving' *Artificial Intelligence*, **2**, 189–208

Forgy, C. L. (1981). *OPS5 User's Manual*. Technical Report CMU-CS-8i-135, Department of Computer Science, Carnegie-Mellon University

Goldberg, A. and Kay, A. (1976). *Smalltalk-72 User's Manual*. Report No. SSL 76-6, Learning Research Group, Xerox PARC, Palo Alto, CA

Goldberg, A. and Robson, D. (1983). *Smalltalk-80: The Language and its Implementation*. Reading, Mass: Addison-Wesley

Grosz, B. J. (1977). *The Representation and Use of Focus in Dialogue Understanding*. Technical Note 151, Stanford Research Institute

Hass, N. and Hendrix, G. (1984). 'Learning by Being Told: Acquiring Knowledge for Information Management' In Michalski, R. S., Carbonell, J. G. and Mitchell, T. M.; Eds. *Machine Learning*. New York: Springer-Verlag

Lenat, D. B. (1982). 'AM: Discovery in Mathematics as Heuristic Search' In Davis, E. R. and Lenat, D. B.; Eds. *Knowledge-Based Systems in Artificial Intelligence*. New York: McGraw-Hill

Marcus, M. P. (1979). 'A Theory of Syntactic Recognition for Natural Language' In Winston, P. H. and Brown, R. H.; Eds. *Artificial Intelligence: An MIT Perspective*. Cambridge, Mass: MIT Press

McDermott, D. V. and Doyle, J. (1980). 'Non-monotonic logic I' *Artificial Intelligence*, **13**, 41–47

Milne, R. W. (1982). 'Predicting Garden Path Sentences' *Cognitive Science*, **6**, 349–373

Minsky, M. (1975). 'A Framework for Representing Knowledge' In Winston, P. H.; Ed. *The Psychology of Computer Vision*. New York: McGraw-Hill

Minsky, M. (1979). *K-Lines: A Theory of Memory*. MIT Artificial Intelligence Laboratory Memo No. 516

Newell, A. and Simon, H. A. (1963). 'GPS: A Program that Simulates Human Thought' In Feigenbaum, E. A. and Fieldman, J.; Eds. *Computers and Thought*. New York: McGraw-Hill

Nilsson, N. J. (1971). *Problem Solving Methods in Artificial Intelligence*. New York: McGraw-Hill

Nilsson, N. J. (1982). *Principles of Artificial Intelligence*. New York: Springer-Verlag

Plyshyn, Z. W. (1984). *Computation and Cognition: Toward a Foundation for Cognitive Science*. Cambridge, Mass: MIT Press

Reiter, R. (1978). 'On Reasoning by Default' *Theoretical Issues in Natural Language Processing*. **2**, 210–218, University of Illinois

Rich, E. (1983). *Artificial Intelligence*. London: McGraw-Hill

Rychener, M. D. (1984). 'The Instructible Production System: A Retrospective Analysis' In Michalski, R. S., Carbonell, J. G. and Mitchell, T. M.; Eds. *Machine Learning*. New York: Springer-Verlag

Sacerdoti, E. D. (1974). 'Planning in a Hierarchy of Abstraction Spaces' *Artificial Intelligence*, **5**, 115–135

Schank, R. C. and Abelson, R. P. (1977). *Scripts, Plans, Goals and Understanding: An Inquiry into Human Knowledge Structures*. Hillsdale NJ: Lawrence Erlbaum

Searle, J. R. (1969). *Speech Acts*. Cambridge: Cambridge University Press

Shortliffe E. H. (1976). *Computer-based Medical Consultations: MYCIN*. New York: Elsevier

Sidner, C. L. (1983). 'Focussing in the Comprehension of Definite Anaphora' In Brady, M. and Berwick, R.; Eds. *Computational Models of Discourse*. Cambridge, Mass: MIT Press

Sowa J. F. (1984). *Conceptual Structures: Information Processing in Mind and Machine*. Reading, Mass: Addison-Wesley

Stallman, R. M. and Sussman, G. J. (1977). 'Forward Reasoning and Dependency-directed Backtracking in a System for Computer-aided Circuit Analysis' *Artificial Intelligence*, **9**, 135–196

Stefik, M. (1981). 'Planning with Constraints (MOLGEN: Part 1)' *Artificial Intelligence*, **16**, 111–139

Swartout, W. R. (1983). 'XPLAIN: a System for Creating and Explaining Expert Consulting Programs' *Artificial Intelligence*, **21**, 285–325

Wanner, E. (1980). 'The ATN and the Sausage Machine: Which one is baloney?' *Cognition*, **8**, 209–225

Wanner, E. and Maratsos, M. P. (1978). 'An ATN Approach to Comprehension' In Halle, M., Bresnan, J. W. and Miller, G. A.; Eds. *Linguistic Theory and Psychological Reality*. Cambridge, Mass: MIT Press

Webber, B. L. (1983). 'So what can we talk about now?' In Brady, M. and Berwick, R.; Eds. *Computational Models of Discourse*. Cambridge, Mass: MIT Press

Welbank, M. (1983). *A Review of Knowledge Acquisition Techniques for Expert Systems*. British Telecom Research, Martlesham Heath, Ipswich

Winograd, T. (1973). 'A Procedural Model of Language Understanding' In Schank, R. C. and Colby, K. M.; Eds. *Computer Models of Thought and Language*. San Francisco: Freeman

Winograd, T. (1983). *Language as a Cognitive Process, Vol. I: Syntax*. Reading, Mass: Addison-Wesley

Winston, P. H. (1975). 'Learning Structural Descriptions from Examples' In Winston, P. H.; Ed. *The Psychology of Computer Vision*. New York: McGraw-Hill

Winston, P. H. (1984). *Artificial Intelligence*. 2nd Edition. Reading, Mass: Addison-Wesley

Winston, P. H. and Horn, B. K. P. (1984). *LISP*. 2nd Edition. Reading, Mass: Addison-Wesley

Woods, W. A. (1970). 'Transition Network Grammars for Natural Language Analysis' *Communications of the ACM*, **13**, 591–606

Index